FOUNDATIONS

A 260-DAY BIBLE READING PLAN FOR BUSY **TEENS**

ROBBY & KANDI GALLATY

REPLIC▲TE   *LifeWay Press® Nashville, Tennessee*

ISBN 9781430064039 Item 005791600
Dewey decimal classification: 242.2 • Subject headings: DEVOTIONAL LITERATURE /
BIBLE STUDY AND TEACHING / GOD

To order additional copies of this resource, write to LifeWay Resources Customer Service;
One LifeWay Plaza; Nashville, TN 37234-0113; fax 615.251.5933; phone toll free
800.458.2772; email *orderentry@lifeway.com*, order online at *www.lifeway.com*, or visit
the LifeWay Christian Store serving you.

Printed in the United States of America

Student Ministry Publishing, LifeWay Resources, One LifeWay Plaza, Nashville, TN
37234-0144

ACKNOWLEDGMENTS

As with any work, many people contributed to make *Foundations* what it is today. First, we are grateful for the tireless hours the Replicate Ministries team members invested. Dave Wiley, Mollie Wiley, Tim LaFleur, John Richardson, and Paul Laso edited, corrected, and organized the reading plan into chronological form. Also, they assisted in selecting memory verses that coincided with each day's reading. Each of you played a crucial role in developing the plan. We couldn't have finished the *Foundations* reading plan without your assistance.

Also, we are appreciative for our partnership with LifeWay. This project would not have become a reality without the support of Bill Craig, Amy Lowe, and Michael Kelley. Thank you for moving forward with the plan. We are particularly grateful for the diligent work of Laura Magness who aided the team in writing the devotional guide material. You have created the bulk of the content for each week's reading.

Finally, we are most thankful for our relationship with God through His Son Jesus Christ. As the walking Word, He has kept us from wandering without direction and guidance. His Word is a lamp to our feet and a light to our path. We are enamored by the truths embedded within the Word for those who take the time to read, meditate, and memorize it.

Our prayer is that many people will develop a passion and love for the Word of God through the daily reading of it.

FOREWORD

One of the foundational elements of becoming a disciple is the process of learning how to interact with and comprehend Scripture on our own.

As a student pastor, one of my greatest desires for students is that they come to a place where the Bible is comfortable in their hands. To truly accomplish this, I make every effort to help students see the power of God's Word in their lives. I also want students to realize the importance of spending time in Scripture every day as a part of their own walk with Christ.

This resource is the perfect tool to facilitate this kind of relationship with God's Word. While it serves as a an excellent guide for reading the Bible daily, the real strength is in the H.E.A.R. method that Robby Gallaty has developed. This is one of the easiest and most effective Bible study methods I have seen.

I encourage you to commit today to learning how to study the Word of God. Take this part of your walk with Christ seriously. Devote time to it every day. Find a friend to journey through this process with you, and hold each other accountable. Then watch as God works in your life to reveal the truth of His Word to you.

John Paul Basham
Manager, LifeWay Student Ministry Publishing

ABOUT THE AUTHORS

ROBBY GALLATY is the Senior Pastor of Long Hollow Baptist Church in Hendersonville, TN. He was radically saved out of a life of drug and alcohol addiction on November 12, 2002. In 2008, he founded Replicate Ministries to educate, equip, and empower men and women to be disciples who make disciple-makers (*www.replicate.org*). He is also the author of *Growing Up: How to Be a Disciple Who Makes Disciples* (B&H Books, 2013), *Firmly Planted: How to Cultivate a Faith Rooted in Christ* (B&H Books, 2015), and *Rediscovering Discipleship: Making Jesus' Final Words Our First Work* (Zondervan, 2015).

KANDI GALLATY has been investing in the lives of women for over a decade. She believes that there are two major sources to draw from when investing in the lives of others: God's Word and God's working in one's life. She is passionate about cultivating a biblical worldview from the truths of Scripture and teaching women how to steward the life experiences and lessons God has allowed in their lives. Kandi and Robby are intentional about investing in their two boys, Rig and Ryder.

LAURA MAGNESS is a content specialist for LifeWay's Discipleship in Context and *smallgroup.com*. She is a graduate of Samford University and Dallas Theological Seminary, and she now lives in Nashville, TN, with her husband and their two young sons.

INTRODUCTION

When I was a new believer, I used the "OPRA" technique for reading the Bible: I would randomly *Open* the Bible, *Point* to a passage, *Read* the verse, and try to figure out a way to *Apply* it to my life. Thankfully, I didn't land on the Scripture that says, "He [speaking of Judas Iscariot] went and hanged himself" (Matt 27:5). Reading random Scriptures will not provide solid biblical growth any more than eating random foods out of your pantry will provide solid physical growth. An effective reading plan is required.

My wife, Kandi, and I recently developed, along with the help of our Replicate team, a reading plan called the Foundational 260. The F-260 is a 260-day reading plan that highlights the foundational passages of Scripture every disciple should know. After failed attempts of reading through the Bible in a year with previous discipleship groups, I wanted a manageable plan that believers who had never read the Bible before could complete.

The plan expects believers to read 1 or 2 chapters a day for 5 days each week, with an allowance for weekends off. The 2 off-days a week are built in so you may catch up on days where you're unable to read. With a traditional reading plan of 4 to 5 chapters a day, unread chapters can begin to pile up, forcing us to skip entire sections to get back on schedule. It reduces Bible reading to a system of box-checking instead of a time to hear from God. The required reading also makes it difficult to sit and reflect on what you've read for that day.

In order to digest more of the Word, the F-260 encourages believers to read less and to keep a H.E.A.R. journal.

HOW DO I LOG A H.E.A.R. JOURNAL ENTRY?

The H.E.A.R. journaling method promotes reading the Bible with a life-transforming purpose. No longer will your focus be on checking off the boxes on your daily reading schedule; your purpose will instead be to read in order to understand and respond to God's Word.

The acronym H.E.A.R. stands for *Highlight*, *Explain*, *Apply*, and *Respond*. Each of these four steps contributes to creating an atmosphere to hear God speak. After settling on a reading plan and establishing a time for studying God's Word, you will be ready to H.E.A.R. from God.

For an illustration, let's assume that you begin your quiet time in the Book of 2 Timothy, and today's reading is the first chapter of the book. Before reading the text, pause to sincerely ask God to speak to you. It may not seem like a big deal, but it is extremely important to seek God's guidance in order to understand His Word (1 Cor. 2:12-14). Every time we open our Bibles, we should pray the simple prayer that David prayed: "Open my eyes so that I may contemplate wonderful things from Your instruction [Word]" (Ps. 119:18).

After praying for the Holy Spirit's guidance, open your notebook or journal, and at the top left-hand corner, write the letter "H." This exercise will remind you to read with a purpose. In the course of your reading, one or two verses will usually stand out and speak to you. After reading the passage of Scripture, *Highlight* each verse that speaks to you by copying it under the letter "H." Write out the following:

- The name of the book

- The passage of Scripture

- The chapter and verse numbers that especially speak to you

- A title to describe the passage

This practice will make it easier to find the passage when you want to revisit it in the future.

After you have highlighted the passage, write the letter "E" under the previous entry. At this stage you will *Explain* what the text means. By asking some simple questions, with the help of God's Spirit, you can understand the meaning of a passage or verse. Here are a few questions to get you started:

- Why was this written?

- To whom was it originally written?

- How does it fit with the verses before and after it?

- Why did the Holy Spirit include this passage in the book?

- What is He intending to communicate through this text?

At this point, you are beginning the process of discovering the specific and personal word that God has for you from His Word. What is important is that you are engaging the text and wrestling with its meaning.

After writing a short summary of what you think the text means, write the letter "A" below the letter "E." Under the "A," write the word *Apply*. This application is the heart of the process. Everything you have done so far culminates under this heading. As you have done before, answer a series of questions to uncover the significance of these verses to you personally — questions like:

- How can this help me?

- What does this mean today?

- What would the application of this verse look like in my life?

- What does this mean to me?

- What is God saying to me?

These questions bridge the gap between the ancient world and your world today. They provide a way for God to speak to you from the specific passage or verse. Answer these questions under the "A." Challenge yourself to write between two and five sentences about how the text applies to your life.

Finally, below the first three entries, write the letter "R" for *Respond*. Your response to the passage may take on many forms. You may write a call to action. You may describe how you will be different because of what God has said to you through His Word. You may indicate what you are going to do because of what you have learned. You may respond by writing out a prayer to God. For example, you may ask God to help you to be more loving, or to give you a desire to be more generous in your giving. Keep in mind that this is your response to what you have just read.

Notice that all of the words in the H.E.A.R. formula are action words: Highlight, Explain, Apply, and Respond. God does not want us to sit back and wait for Him to drop some truth into our laps. Instead of waiting passively, God desires that we actively pursue Him. Jesus said,

"Keep asking, and it will be given to you. Keep searching, and you will find. Keep knocking, and the door will be opened to you" (Matt. 7:7).

Think of the miracle of the Bible. Over centuries of time, God supernaturally moved upon a number of men in an unusual way that resulted in them writing the exact words of God. God led His people to recognize these divine writings and to distinguish them from everything else that has ever been written. Then God's people brought these sixty-six books together. The preservation and survival of the Bible is as miraculous as its writing. Then God gave men, beginning with Gutenberg's printing press, technological knowledge to copy and transmit the Bible so that all people could have it. All because God has something to say to you.

MEMORIZING THE WORD

While many plans for memorizing Scripture are effective, a simple system has been effective for me. All you need is a pack of index cards and a committed desire to memorize God's Word. It's easy: write the reference of the verse on one side of the card and the text of the verse on the other. Focus on five verses at a time, and carry your pack of Scripture cards with you.

Throughout the day, whenever you have a few minutes, pull out your pack of Scripture cards and review them. Read the reference first, followed by the verse. Continue to recite the verse until you get a feel for the flow of the passage. When you are comfortable with the text, look only at the reference side of the card in order to test your recall.

It is important to recite the reference first, then the verse, and finish with the reference again. This will prevent you from becoming a concordance cripple. As a new believer, I was forced to look up every verse in the concordance at the back of my Bible. Sometimes, when I quoted a Scripture while witnessing, the person would ask me, "Where did you get that?" I could only respond, "Somewhere in the Bible." As you can imagine, that is not effective when sharing with others! By memorizing the references, you will speak with authority and gain the respect of your hearers when you quote Scripture.

When you master five verses, begin to study five more. Review all of the verses you have learned at least once a week. As your pack grows, you will be encouraged to keep going in Scripture memorization, and you will experience its powerful effects in your life.

For an example of a H.E.A.R. entry, refer to page 272. For disciple-making resources check out our website: *www.replicate.org*

1//GENESIS 1–2

MEMORY VERSES: GENESIS 1:27; HEBREWS 11:7

A person's worldview is defined by how they see or think about the world. The first two chapters of the Bible establish the biblical worldview all Christians should have when it comes to how they think about the natural world, human identity, and human relationships. These chapters affirm God as a sovereign, loving Creator, speaking the natural world into existence for His glory. He made humans in His image, linking our identity to His own. He also made male and female as partners who complement one another and model unity within the diversity that is found in the body of Christ.

As you read the Bible this week...

HIGHLIGHT the verses that speak to you.

Genesis 1:27 Hebrews 11:7

Which chapter and verse numbers stand out to you?

EXPLAIN what this passage means.

Everyones perfect In his eyes because he made them

How does it fit with the verses before and after it?

What is the Holy Spirit intending to communicate through this text?

APPLY what God is saying in these verses to your life.

We were created perfectly by god

What is God saying to you personally?

How can you apply this message to your life?

RESPOND to what you've read.

If you disrespect yourself your dis-respecting god

How is your life different because of what you've learned?

Write out a prayer to God in response to what you read today:

2//GENESIS 3–4

GENESIS 1:27; HEBREWS 11:7 *One fruit ruined it all for us.*

In these two chapters, we read how God's perfect creation was made imperfect through the cunning deceit of the serpent, or Satan, one of God's own creations who rebelled against Him. The serpent convinced Eve to doubt God's goodness, and in response she disobeyed God and convinced Adam to do the same. We know this event as the fall of man. With that single act of disobedience, sin entered the world. The negative impact of sin is felt in all of creation. Through Adam and Eve, sin became an inevitable part of human nature.

H

E

A

R

3//GENESIS 6–7

MEMORY VERSES: GENESIS 1:27; HEBREWS 11:7

It didn't take long for sin to wreak havoc on God's perfect creation. Notice how quickly the human race spiraled in its immorality and corruption. Humanity was created to worship and obey God, and because that no longer took place, God acted in judgment against the world's sin by sending a flood to wipe out the entire human race. In as much as God is just, though, these chapters also give evidence of His mercy through the fact that Noah and his family found favor in God's eyes. He, subsequently, spared their lives. All of Scripture affirms that these two aspects of God's character—His justice and mercy—remain in perfect harmony at all times.

H

E

A

R

4//GENESIS 8–9

Genesis 8–9 record the aftermath of the flood. Noah and his family faithfully obeyed God, and God faithfully protected them from His judgment. We are reminded of God's love for humans—those He created in His own image. God used Noah's family to once again populate the earth with His people. In what is known as the Noahic covenant, God promised to never again destroy the earth and its inhabitants with a flood—a promise He has kept to this day. God sealed this promise with a rainbow, a sign that God keeps His promises.

H
_____

E
_____
_____
_____

A
_____
_____
_____
_____

R
_____
_____
_____
_____
_____

5//JOB 1–2

MEMORY VERSES: GENESIS 1:27; HEBREWS 11:7

The Book of Job addresses the issue of why God allows suffering in the lives of His people. The early chapters of Genesis describe sin's entrance into and corruption of the world. We also realize that human suffering is an inevitable consequence of sin. Job 1–2 remind us that even the most faithful of God's people are not exempt from suffering and sin. However, these chapters also remind us that because God is sovereign, everything—even suffering—has a purpose that ultimately leads to His glory and the fulfillment of His plans. The purpose of Job's suffering was that the world would see the life-transforming power of genuine faith in God.

H

E

A

R

6//JOB 38–39

MEMORY VERSES: HEBREWS 11:6; HEBREWS 11:8-10

Last week's reading ended with Job 1–2, which describes the suffering God allowed Job to endure as a way for God to be glorified. In chapters 3–37, Job wrestled with his despair both privately and in the company of friends. In Job 38, God finally speaks. His words to Job were a reminder that the One Job questioned was the Almighty Creator and Sustainer of the universe. Job's story reveals that God is in control, His ways are best, and everything exists to bring glory to Him.

As you read the Bible this week...

HIGHLIGHT the verses that speak to you.

Write out the name of the book:

Which chapter and verse numbers stand out to you?

EXPLAIN what this passage means.

To whom was it originally written? Why?

How does it fit with the verses before and after it?

What is the Holy Spirit intending to communicate through this text?

APPLY what God is saying in these verses to your life.

What does this mean today?

What is God saying to you personally?

How can you apply this message to your life?

RESPOND to what you've read.

In what ways does this passage call you to action?

How will you be different because of what you've learned?

Write out a prayer to God in response to what you read today:

7//JOB 40–42

MEMORY VERSES: HEBREWS 11:6; HEBREWS 11:8-10

After being reminded of God's holiness and power, Job could do nothing but confess his sins, turn back to God, and renew his trust in the Lord. He humbly said, "I ... repent in dust and ashes" (Job 42:6). In the face of God's holiness, we are reminded that apart from Him, we are nothing but dust from the ground, and to dust we will return (Gen. 2:7). Yet through Job's experience, we are reminded that God gives physical life through His very breath, and He gives spiritual life through the death and resurrection of His Son. These are gifts we do not deserve, and they motivate us to imitate Job's practice of confession and repentance, continually removing anything from our hearts, thoughts, and lives that keeps us from trusting God in all things.

H

E

A

R

7//JOB 40–42

8//GENESIS 11–12

MEMORY VERSES: HEBREWS 11:6; HEBREWS 11:8-10

Through Noah's family, the earth was repopulated after the flood, and Genesis 11 states that people shared a common language and a common goal—making a name for themselves. As had happened twice before in Genesis 3–10, people who were created by God to glorify Him put their efforts toward glorifying themselves instead. And yet again, humanity's sin brought God's judgment. But despite the people's continued sinfulness, we see God's covenant love for humanity through the promise He made with Abram in Genesis 12—a promise to bless all the people of the earth through Himself. This promise ultimately found its fulfillment in Jesus Christ, who descended through the genealogical line of Abram, and through whom all people have access to the grace and redemption of God.

H

E

A

R

9//GENESIS 15

God promised to make Abram into a great nation, but Abram and his wife were childless. While Abram waited for God to fulfill His promise, years went by and still no children came. Then God spoke to Abram again, this time making an even more specific promise that Abram would have a son, which would then lead to offspring as numerous as the stars. Genesis 15:6 says that despite the prolonged years of barrenness, Abram believed God, and that belief made him righteous, or put him in a right relationship with God. Likewise, when we believe the gospel—the death and resurrection of Jesus for our salvation—God considers us righteous, too.

H

E

A

R

10//GENESIS 16–17

MEMORY VERSES: HEBREWS 11:6; HEBREWS 11:8-10

In Genesis 16, the focus shifts from Abram to his wife, Sarai. All they knew of God's promise was that they would have an heir, so Sarai took the initiative to provide that heir herself by using Hagar, her servant, as a surrogate mother. Sarai's actions revealed a lack of trust in God's ability to provide. God alone was the engineer of Abram and Sarai's destiny, and their attempts to go about it without God paled in comparison to the grandeur of His plan. Once more in Genesis 17, God reminded Abram that He would be the one to bless them, He would give them the promised son, Isaac, He would make their descendants as numerous as the stars, and He would receive all of the glory. God's faithfulness and ability to do what He says overcomes all of our flaws and uncertainties.

H

E

A

R

11//GENESIS 18–19

MEMORY VERSES: ROMANS 4:20-22; HEBREWS 11:17-19

In Genesis 18, three visitors appeared to Abraham and reaffirmed God's promise to give Abraham and Sarah a son. Just before the visitors left, Abraham learned that God was about to judge the cities of Sodom and Gomorrah for their sins. Abraham questioned God's mercy and justice, and when God stated that He would spare the city for 10 righteous people, Abraham understood the extent of God's love and mercy (18:22-33). Unfortunately, God already knew that 10 righteous people would not be found in the city, and chapter 19 records the destruction that came to them as a result. Sin is a violation of the very character of God, and because He is just, He must take action against it. Thankfully, the finality of God's action against sin took place at the cross, when Jesus bore God's wrath for our sin once and for all.

As you read the Bible this week...

H I G H L I G H T the verses that speak to you.

Write out the name of the book:

Which chapter and verse numbers stand out to you?

E X P L A I N what this passage means.

To whom was it originally written? Why?

How does it fit with the verses before and after it?

What is the Holy Spirit intending to communicate through this text?

A P P L Y what God is saying in these verses to your life.

What does this mean today?

What is God saying to you personally?

How can you apply this message to your life?

R E S P O N D to what you've read.

In what ways does this passage call you to action?

How will you be different because of what you've learned?

Write out a prayer to God in response to what you read today:

12//GENESIS 20–21

Despite God's continued faithfulness, Abraham still had a hard time learning to trust God in all things. Afraid for his life, Abraham lied about Sarah's identity as his wife and put the entire kingdom in jeopardy. Even so, God's faithfulness to His covenant promises shone through as He protected Abraham in spite of his sin. Next, as God had promised, Sarah became pregnant by Abraham and delivered a son at the exact time God had specified. These two chapters speak to God's promise-keeping nature. Thankfully, as Abraham's life demonstrates, God is faithful to His promises no matter how many times His children sin and stumble. God's love outweighs even our biggest weaknesses.

H

E

A

R

13//GENESIS 22

MEMORY VERSES: ROMANS 4:20-22; HEBREWS 11:17-19

The story of Abraham's testing in Genesis 22 is one of the most famous stories about his life. After waiting years for God to fulfill His promise of a son, imagine Abraham's shock when God asked him to sacrifice his "only son" to Him. Immediately Abraham set off to obey God in faith, but as Abraham prepared to sacrifice his son, God stopped him and provided a sacrificial ram in Isaac's place. Abraham's willingness to sacrifice his son in obedience to God reminds us how God has done the same for us. God gave His "only Son," Jesus, to die for us as a sacrifice for our sins. If God is willing to sacrifice the One He loves most, why would we not offer everything, even our lives, as living sacrifices back to Him (Rom. 12:1-2)?

H

E

A

R

14//GENESIS 24

MEMORY VERSES: ROMANS 4:20-22; HEBREWS 11:17-19

Time and again throughout Abraham's story, we see God faithfully keep the promises He made to Abraham. One of those promises was that Abraham's offspring would inherit the land of Canaan, which became known as the promised land (Gen. 12:7). Realizing he was getting old, Abraham planned for Isaac's future. He summoned a servant and sent him to find a wife for Isaac. Abraham was confident that God's hand would guide them, so his servant also trusted that it would happen, and it did. Through a series of events, God revealed that Rebekah was to be Isaac's future wife. This part of Abraham's story reminds us that our all-knowing, all-powerful God is continually at work in and through us to accomplish His good purposes.

H

E

A

R

15//GENESIS 25:19-34; 26

MEMORY VERSES: ROMANS 4:20-22; HEBREWS 11:17-19

Isaac married Rebekah, and like Sarah, it appeared Rebekah would be childless. But after Isaac prayed to God, she gave birth to twin boys—Esau and Jacob. Early on, animosity ran deep between these two brothers. One day, when Esau came home exhausted from an unsuccessful hunt, Jacob sold him a bowl of soup in exchange for Esau's birthright, the first recorded instance of what would become a life-long sibling rivalry rooted in jealousy and pride. These were Isaac's sons, so they, too, were children of the promise—God's covenant with Abraham. And like the covenant He had with Abraham, God promised to bless Isaac and his offspring. By pointing out many of Isaac's, Jacob's, and Esau's sins, the writer of Genesis (Moses) reminds us again that God's faithfulness to and love of His people has nothing to do with them and has everything to do with Him.

H

E

A

R

16//GENESIS 27–28

MEMORY VERSES: 2 CORINTHIANS 10:12; 1 JOHN 3:18

When Isaac was old and blind, Jacob deceived him, causing Isaac to give Jacob the family blessing instead of Esau, the older son to whom it rightfully belonged. Esau responded with anger and murderous thoughts, so Jacob had no choice but to escape and seek refuge with extended family, at which time he also sought out a wife. As God had with Isaac and Abraham, He spoke to Jacob at the start of his journey and reiterated His covenant promises for their family. With that event, Jacob's life took a turn away from the deception and selfishness of his youth and toward his future as a faithful patriarch who would lead his family to trust in the Lord. God's promise to Jacob—"I am with you and will keep you" (28:15, ESV)—remains His life-changing promise to us today through the once-for-all sacrifice of Jesus.

As you read the Bible this week...

H IGHLIGHT the verses that speak to you.

Write out the name of the book:

Which chapter and verse numbers stand out to you?

E XPLAIN what this passage means.

To whom was it originally written? Why?

How does it fit with the verses before and after it?

What is the Holy Spirit intending to communicate through this text?

A PPLY what God is saying in these verses to your life.

What does this mean today?

What is God saying to you personally?

How can you apply this message to your life?

R ESPOND to what you've read.

In what ways does this passage call you to action?

How will you be different because of what you've learned?

Write out a prayer to God in response to what you read today:

17//GENESIS 29–30:24

MEMORY VERSES: 2 CORINTHIANS 10:12; 1 JOHN 3:18

The beginning of Jacob's own family and the birth of several of his children is documented in the next several chapters of Genesis. Deception and envy are two key issues that ran throughout this family's relationships. Jacob deceived his father and his brother, then found himself on the receiving end of deception from Laban, who promised Jacob one daughter in marriage, but tricked him into marrying another. Eventually, Jacob married both Leah and Rachel, and their ability and inability (respectively) to have children became the source of yet more jealousy and envy. As is God's providential nature, from these corrupted relationships came twelve sons who eventually became the heads of the twelve tribes of Israel. Even better, one of those tribes—the tribe of Judah—would eventually bring forth the Messiah, God's promised deliverer of His people, Jesus Christ our Redeemer.

H

E

A

R

18//GENESIS 31–32

MEMORY VERSES: 2 CORINTHIANS 10:12; 1 JOHN 3:18

As a result of God's grace and power in his life, Jacob experienced great prosperity during these years, which became yet another source of jealousy among his extended family. Again God appeared to Jacob in a dream, this time urging Jacob to take his family and return home to Canaan. When Jacob and his family left, Laban pursued them, but God again proved faithful to protect and deliver Jacob from harm. Unfortunately, "home" did not hold the promise of peace for Jacob either because he was returning to his brother Esau, who in their last encounter threatened to kill Jacob. Genesis 32 highlights the anxiety Jacob felt, which led to an unexpected encounter with God. From Jacob's "wrestling match" with God, we are reminded that God will go to great lengths in order to teach us to depend on Him and trust the sufficiency of His grace.

H

E

A

R

19//GENESIS 33; 35

MEMORY VERSES: 2 CORINTHIANS 10:12; 1 JOHN 3:18

The reunion of Jacob and Esau is one of the greatest pictures of reconciliation in the Bible (Gen. 33). Enough time and life experience had passed between the two brothers that the grudges of their youth were forgotten, and Jacob noted, "I have seen your face, and it is like seeing God's face" (33:10). Only the Lord's work in their lives could bring about such change. Through that reunion and some other horrific events described in Genesis 34, Jacob realized that he and his family needed to renew their commitment to the Lord. Genesis 35 describes that renewal of their commitment to God and God's covenant promises to them. Scripture is filled with many promises from God that still apply to His children today. Regularly strengthening our commitment to God and trusting Him to keep His promises is a vital part of following Christ.

H

E

A

R

20//GENESIS 37

MEMORY VERSES: 2 CORINTHIANS 10:12; 1 JOHN 3:18

With Genesis 37, the story of God's chosen people shifts from Jacob to his son Joseph, who is the main character throughout the rest of Genesis. Rachel struggled to have children, and Joseph was the first child she was able to bear. Because Rachel was Jacob's favorite wife, Joseph became Jacob's favorite son, which meant blessings from his father and ridicule from his brothers. In what has become one of the most well-known accounts in the Old Testament, Joseph was sold into slavery by his brothers, who then lied to their father by telling him Joseph was dead. This set in motion a series of trials Joseph would face over many years, but early on in his story, we see evidence that God was orchestrating the events of Joseph's life. God gave Joseph the power to interpret dreams, a divine gift that would determine the course his life would take to protect God's covenant people.

H

E

A

R

21//GENESIS 39–40

MEMORY VERSES: ROMANS 8:28-30; EPHESIANS 3:20-21

Joseph's brothers sold him as a slave to the Midianites, who took Joseph to Egypt where he was sold to Potiphar, an officer of Pharaoh. Potiphar soon came to respect Joseph, and over time Joseph's authority in Potiphar's house increased. Unfortunately, Joseph's loyalty to Potiphar resulted in an attempted seduction by his master's wife. The short-term result was Joseph's undeserved imprisonment. Yet, in spite of this and other setbacks, Joseph knew God was with him, and the opportunity to put his God-given gift of dream interpretation to work further supported God's active presence in Joseph's life.

As you read the Bible this week...

H I G H L I G H T the verses that speak to you.

Write out the name of the book:

Which chapter and verse numbers stand out to you?

E X P L A I N what this passage means.

To whom was it originally written? Why?

How does it fit with the verses before and after it?

What is the Holy Spirit intending to communicate through this text?

A P P L Y what God is saying in these verses to your life.

What does this mean today?

What is God saying to you personally?

How can you apply this message to your life?

R E S P O N D to what you've read.

In what ways does this passage call you to action?

How will you be different because of what you've learned?

Write out a prayer to God in response to what you read today:

22//GENESIS 41

MEMORY VERSES: ROMANS 8:28-30; EPHESIANS 3:20-21

In Genesis 41, God's sovereignty is on display through Joseph's story in several key ways. God prepared Joseph to interpret Pharaoh's dream and positioned him at the appropriate time to do so. God put plans in place that enabled the Egyptians and others to survive the famine. God orchestrated Joseph's rise in power. Despite the actions of people like Joseph's brothers and Potiphar's wife, God put Joseph in a position where he would be able to protect and provide for God's covenant people.

H

E

A

R

23//GENESIS 42–43

MEMORY VERSES: ROMANS 8:28-30; EPHESIANS 3:20-21

The famine Joseph predicted from Pharaoh's dreams came to be, and its impact reached beyond Egypt even to Canaan, Joseph's homeland. In another demonstration of God's providence, Joseph's rise in power, combined with the horrific effects of the famine in Canaan, brought Joseph and his brothers together: Joseph controlled the distribution of grain for the region, and Jacob sent his sons to Egypt to buy some of that grain. Joseph's brothers did not recognize him, so he put an intricate plan for reunion in place. At the heart of Joseph's plan was a desire to see his father again and be reconciled to his brothers.

H

E

A

R

24//GENESIS 44–45

MEMORY VERSES: ROMANS 8:28-30; EPHESIANS 3:20-21

Joseph's reunion with his brothers brought to light the maturity and compassion that had developed in them since their last meeting. When Joseph was sold into slavery, Judah orchestrated the events (Gen. 37). But when Benjamin was threatened with slavery, Judah offered his own life as a sacrifice in Benjamin's place because he knew the pain that losing Benjamin would cause his father (Gen. 44). With this, Joseph knew his brothers had changed, and he could hide his identity no longer. The forgiveness and compassion Joseph showed his brothers is a picture of the forgiveness and compassion God has shown us in Christ. Even though we have sinned against God, He loves us and made the ultimate sacrifice to draw us back to Himself.

H

E

A

R

25//GENESIS 46–47

MEMORY VERSES: ROMANS 8:28-30; EPHESIANS 3:20-21

The same famine that brought Joseph to power also brought his family to Egypt (47:4). By moving the family to Egypt, Jacob (whom God renamed Israel) was reunited with his long lost son. Through Joseph's faithfulness to God and loyalty to Pharaoh, he was able to make a way for his family to settle in the land and escape the worst effects of the famine. Beyond that, Joseph also managed to keep Pharaoh prosperous and keep people fed during a tragic time in Egypt's history. Yet again, God used an international disaster and the faithfulness of one person to advance His purposes for His covenant people.

H

E

A

R

26//GENESIS 48–49

MEMORY VERSES: GENESIS 50:20; HEBREWS 11:24-26

Joseph's story paints one big picture of God's faithfulness to His children and His promises. In these chapters, we see several examples of God's work through the lives of Jacob's family. Genesis 48 describes how Jacob adopted Manasseh and Ephraim, Joseph's Egyptian sons, into their family, which was the covenant family of God. When Jacob took them as his own sons (Gen. 48:5), he guaranteed that Joseph and his descendants would be a part of God's covenant community in the generations to come. Jesus' crucifixion and resurrection accomplished a similar purpose. Through the death and resurrection of Jesus, anyone who believes in Jesus becomes an adopted child of God and heir to all His promises (Rom. 8:12-17).

As you read the Bible this week...

H I G H L I G H T the verses that speak to you.

Write out the name of the book:

Which chapter and verse numbers stand out to you?

E X P L A I N what this passage means.

To whom was it originally written? Why?

How does it fit with the verses before and after it?

What is the Holy Spirit intending to communicate through this text?

A P P L Y what God is saying in these verses to your life.

What does this mean today?

What is God saying to you personally?

How can you apply this message to your life?

R E S P O N D to what you've read.

In what ways does this passage call you to action?

How will you be different because of what you've learned?

Write out a prayer to God in response to what you read today:

27//GENESIS 50—EXODUS 1

MEMORY VERSES: GENESIS 50:20; HEBREWS 11:24-26

Fearing for their lives after Jacob's death, Joseph's brothers sought forgiveness and offered to be his slaves. Joseph then revealed his understanding that everything that had happened to him was part of God's larger plan (Gen. 50:20). In spite of all the hardships Joseph had suffered, God had positioned him perfectly to do the most good for the greatest number of people. Genesis 50:20 is one of the Bible's clearest affirmations of God's sovereignty—the fact that all things are under God's control and nothing happens apart from His plan and purpose. However, it wasn't long before that belief and the faithfulness of God's people was put to the test, as Exodus 1 describes. After Joseph died, the Israelites in Egypt were forced into slavery, and Pharaoh demanded all newborn baby boys be killed in order to keep the Israelite population from growing. Once again the stage was set for God to act on behalf of His people in order to bring glory to His name.

H

E

A

R

28//EXODUS 2–3

Throughout the Bible, God calls individual people to play key roles in His redemptive plan, such as Noah, Abraham, Joseph, and Moses. God protected Moses following his birth because of the plans He had for Moses, and Moses grew up as an Egyptian prince. However, Moses' murderous action against an Egyptian slave forced him out of the land and into a new life in Midian, where he married and became a shepherd. It was there that Moses' famous "burning bush" encounter with God took place. When the Egyptian king died, the Israelites cried out to God for deliverance. He heard them and acted to save them. Using a burning bush to get Moses' attention, God called him to lead the Israelites out of slavery. At that time, God also revealed to Moses His name—Yahweh, "I AM WHO I AM." One of the great truths about God is that He does not change, a fact tied up in His very identity and name. This helps us know that just as God was faithful in the lives of His Old Testament servants, He continues to prove Himself faithful to us today.

H

E

A

R

29//EXODUS 4–5

MEMORY VERSES: GENESIS 50:20; HEBREWS 11:24-26

God had big plans for Moses, but Moses was not convinced God picked the right man for the job. Moses voiced hesitation at what God asked of him, so God gave him three signs and promised to send his brother Aaron to assist him. Each of the signs—turning the staff into a snake, turning Moses' hand leprous, and turning water into blood—revealed God's power over the created world, which reminded Moses and all the Israelites that God also had the power to set them free. Convinced that he should obey God, Moses met up with Aaron, and the two assembled the Israelites and showed them God's signs. As a result, the people worshiped God, thanking Him for hearing their prayers (4:18-31). However, they had a long road to freedom. Chapter 5 describes Moses' and Aaron's first meeting with Pharaoh, who responded to their request for freedom by denying God's existence and making life for the Israelites even more difficult.

H

E

A

R

30//EXODUS 6–7

MEMORY VERSES: GENESIS 50:20; HEBREWS 11:24-26

When God called Moses, the plan was to use Moses to set the Israelites free. Yet in the eyes of the Israelites, that plan seemed to backfire. When Moses complained to God, God reminded Moses of His connection to Abraham, Isaac, and Jacob and reaffirmed His covenant with them. He promised to deliver the Israelites and to bring them to a new land, the promised land. God revealed that prolonging the Israelites' suffering had a purpose, just like the sufferings of Joseph and Job. Since Pharaoh would not let the Israelites go, God would bring His people out by His power. Through His wondrous acts, the Egyptians would see the glory of God. Pharaoh's continued refusal to free God's people brought about ten plagues, the first of which was the plague of blood. One must not miss the great truth about God tucked away in Exodus 6. In God's reassurance to Moses, He described the process of revelation and redemption by which all people are saved: "I will deliver you ... I will redeem you ... I will take you as My people, and I will be your God" (6:6-7). Here again the cross of Christ was foreshadowed.

H

E

A

R

31//EXODUS 8–9

MEMORY VERSES: JOHN 1:29; HEBREWS 9:22

Because Pharaoh refused to listen to Moses and free the Israelites, God unleashed a series of ten plagues on the nation. The water in the Nile River turned to blood. Then frogs, gnats, and flies overran the land. One plague caused the death of livestock. Another brought boils, while another was a plague of deadly hail. As with everything God does, the goal of the plagues was that the Egyptians would see His glory on display. Moses announced each plague, and each arrived and departed exactly as he stated. These announcements served as warnings to Pharaoh, and they gave him the opportunity to act. They also gave a testimony to God's grace. His plagues weren't set in stone, and had Pharaoh acknowledged God and freed His people, God would have extended grace to Pharaoh and the nation. However, Pharaoh would not relent. The plagues punished Egypt, showed the powerlessness of their gods, and demonstrated God's glory.

As you read the Bible this week...

HIGHLIGHT the verses that speak to you.

Write out the name of the book:

Which chapter and verse numbers stand out to you?

EXPLAIN what this passage means.

To whom was it originally written? Why?

How does it fit with the verses before and after it?

What is the Holy Spirit intending to communicate through this text?

APPLY what God is saying in these verses to your life.

What does this mean today?

What is God saying to you personally?

How can you apply this message to your life?

RESPOND to what you've read.

In what ways does this passage call you to action?

How will you be different because of what you've learned?

Write out a prayer to God in response to what you read today:

32//EXODUS 10–11

MEMORY VERSES: JOHN 1:29; HEBREWS 9:22

Exodus 10–11 describe the final three plagues—a swarm of locusts, darkness that descended over all of Egypt, and the plague on the firstborn males in the Egyptian households. As with the previous plagues, Pharaoh initially repented, but changed his mind after God withdrew the plague from the land. However, God told Moses He would send one final plague, and after that the people would be free. Again, the goal of the plagues was that everyone, the Israelites and the Egyptians, would recognize the power and glory of God. That's why He went into such detail with Moses' instructions in the first place. God left no room for doubt as to who was in control. Exodus 11:5-7 reveals God's plan to protect the firstborn sons of the Israelites, further evidence that He would protect His people and continue to uphold His covenant with Abraham.

H

E

A

R

33//EXODUS 12

MEMORY VERSES: JOHN 1:29; HEBREWS 9:22

On the night of the plague on the firstborn Egyptians, God established Passover—a Jewish holiday that commemorates God's deliverance of the Israelites from Egypt. Passover got its name from the animal blood smeared on the door posts, which marked the Israelites apart from the Egyptians and served as a sign for God's angelic death to "pass over" the house without killing the firstborn. Once the plague came down on the people, Pharaoh summoned Moses and ordered the Israelites to leave. With that, the Israelites began their exodus journey. Centuries later, Jesus Christ became the ultimate Passover Lamb when God sent Him to be the sacrifice to save people from the bondage of their sins once and for all. In Jesus, all of the ritual aspects of the Passover described in Exodus 12 find their fulfillment.

H

E

A

R

34//EXODUS 13:17–14

MEMORY VERSES: JOHN 1:29; HEBREWS 9:22

God's presence accompanied the Israelites from the very beginning of their exodus journey, as symbolized by the pillars of cloud and fire that led them on their way. The Israelites had not been out of Egypt long, though, when their fate seemed to take a turn for the worse. Once again God hardened Pharaoh's heart, and Pharaoh gathered an army to track down the Israelites. Exodus 14 makes it clear that this was all a part of God's plan. Moses encouraged the people to trust God, and this encounter culminated in the most famous event in the exodus—the parting of the Red Sea. Moses stretched his hand over the sea, God divided the waters, and the Israelites crossed on dry ground. When the Egyptians pursued the Israelites across the dry sea floor, God brought the waters back together, drowning Pharaoh's army. With that single act, God acted in final judgment against Pharaoh, and the Israelites feared God and believed in Him (14:31).

H

E

A

R

35//EXODUS 16–17

MEMORY VERSES: JOHN 1:29; HEBREWS 9:22

The Israelites were free from slavery, but they were not free from hardship. God used this to test their dependence on and obedience to Him. With food difficult to find in the wilderness, the Israelites remembered the days of Egyptian slavery when they at least had enough to eat. The people complained to Moses, and God responded by sending quail and manna—daily provisions of food to sustain them on their journey. God met the people's need for food (and then again for water in chapter 17), again revealing His care and provisions for His people. By sending the food daily, the people had no choice but to remain dependent on Him, something they struggled to do despite all the ways He had already provided for them. This struggle with trust would be the defining characteristic of the Israelites' 40 years in the desert, and it is a good reminder for us when our trust in God waivers or we forget how faithful He truly is. Just as God provided water and food to sustain the Israelites, He has given us Jesus to forever quench the hunger and thirst of our souls (John 4).

H

E

A

R

36//EXODUS 19–20

MEMORY VERSES: EXODUS 20:1-3; GALATIANS 5:14

Following God's miraculous work to get His people out of Egypt, the Israelites journeyed through the desert, eventually setting up camp at Mount Sinai. On that mountain, God spoke to Moses, telling him that if the Israelites would remember what He had done and obey Him, they would demonstrate that they were His special and holy people. God made good on His promise to Abraham to make a great nation out of Abraham's descendants, then He gave them the Ten Commandments to help them know how to live as His chosen people. The first four commandments focused on the people's relationship with God, while the next six focused on the people's relationships with one another. The ultimate goal of the Ten Commandments was to highlight the people's need for God and point them toward holiness.

As you read the Bible this week...

HIGHLIGHT the verses that speak to you.

Write out the name of the book:

Which chapter and verse numbers stand out to you?

EXPLAIN what this passage means.

To whom was it originally written? Why?

How does it fit with the verses before and after it?

What is the Holy Spirit intending to communicate through this text?

APPLY what God is saying in these verses to your life.

What does this mean today?

What is God saying to you personally?

How can you apply this message to your life?

RESPOND to what you've read.

In what ways does this passage call you to action?

How will you be different because of what you've learned?

Write out a prayer to God in response to what you read today:

37//EXODUS 24–25

MEMORY VERSES: EXODUS 20:1-3; GALATIANS 5:14

In Exodus 21–23, God gave the Israelites further instructions for worship and living. Then the Israelites made a covenant with God in which they promised to obey Him. The ritual sacrifice Moses performed to seal the covenant foreshadowed the death of Jesus on the cross—the animal's blood was shed as a sacrifice for the sins of the people, which made a way for them to unite with God in this covenant. Following the dictation of the Law, God next laid out very specific instructions for the building of a tabernacle, a place set aside for His presence to dwell, in which they could worship Him regularly. Chapter 25 gives details for the ark, the table, and the lampstand. Each item was intentionally designed to point the worshipers to God, and they were made of a wide range of natural materials, meaning everyone was able to give an offering to help build the sanctuary (25:1-9). Giving is built into our relationship with God as an act of worship.

H

E

A

R

38//EXODUS 26–27

MEMORY VERSES: EXODUS 20:1-3; GALATIANS 5:14

The tabernacle was a large tent used for gathering to worship. Because of the way God designed it, the tabernacle could be taken apart and carried as the people continued on their journey to the promised land. The tent served as a reminder of God's constant presence and their need to center life on Him, no matter where they went. The veil of the tabernacle, described in Exodus 26:31-35, separated the ark of the covenant and the mercy seat of God from the rest of the tabernacle and all the people. In other words, it separated the people from the presence of God. This is why it's so significant that when Jesus died on the cross, the veil was ripped in two (Luke 23:45). Jesus' sacrifice made access to God possible for all people, as it still does today.

H

E

A

R

39//EXODUS 28–29

Along with the instructions God gave Moses for building the tabernacle and its components, He also provided instructions for the creation of the priestly garments—particularly the robes, ephod, and breast-piece worn by the high priest. Once the tabernacle had been constructed and furnished and the priestly garments had been created, everything needed to be dedicated and consecrated for worship. As part of that, God asked the people to give Him their best as an offering, and doing so became a regular part of their faith in and obedience to Him. As it did for the Israelites, giving God our best, not what's left over, honors Him and shows our gratitude to Him for giving us His best through Christ.

H

E

A

R

40//EXODUS 30–31

MEMORY VERSES: EXODUS 20:1-3; GALATIANS 5:14

As God wrapped up His instructions for the tabernacle, He described the Day of Atonement—one day a year in which the high priest made a sacrifice on behalf of the sins of all the Israelites. The writer of Hebrews tells us that the Day of Atonement pointed forward to the sacrifice of Jesus, whose death on the cross cleanses us from our sins once and for all (Heb. 9:24-28). Before appointing men to head up the building projects, God told the people to contribute money to the project. God's final instruction to the people was a reminder not to work on the Sabbath. Building a place for worship was going to take a lot of work, but it did not exclude the people from worship itself.

H

E

A

R

41//EXODUS 32–33

MEMORY VERSES: EXODUS 33:16; MATTHEW 22:37-39

The Israelites were guided by God's presence through the desert and heard Him speak to Moses on Mount Sinai, but even those awe-inspiring encounters with God did not keep them from sinning. Moses' prolonged absence from the Israelites—while he was on the mountain receiving instructions from God—led them to demand Aaron make a representation of God. Taking gold earrings from the women and children, Aaron made a golden calf, and the people held a great feast sacrificing to this idol. Like the people the apostle Paul condemned in Romans 1, the Israelites preferred to worship created things rather than the Creator Himself. In response to this sin, God threatened to destroy the people, but Moses interceded on their behalf, leading God to spare them. Our sin, too, warrants death, but Jesus interceded on our behalf, and the wrath that we earned was poured out on Him as He hung on the cross.

As you read the Bible this week...

HIGHLIGHT the verses that speak to you.

Write out the name of the book:

Which chapter and verse numbers stand out to you?

EXPLAIN what this passage means.

To whom was it originally written? Why?

How does it fit with the verses before and after it?

What is the Holy Spirit intending to communicate through this text?

APPLY what God is saying in these verses to your life.

What does this mean today?

What is God saying to you personally?

How can you apply this message to your life?

RESPOND to what you've read.

In what ways does this passage call you to action?

How will you be different because of what you've learned?

Write out a prayer to God in response to what you read today:

42//EXODUS 34–36:1

Out of anger for the people's idolatry, Moses broke the first pair of stone tablets on which God had inscribed His Commandments. But as has been proven throughout Genesis and Exodus, God's faithfulness to His people is not based on their actions; it is rooted solely in His character. God renewed His covenant with Moses and inscribed a new set of tablets. When Moses ascended Mount Sinai again, God declared His Name and nature, causing Moses to worship Him. In chapter 33, Moses asked to see God's glory, and on the mountain God granted him that request. When Moses came down from the mountain, his face shown with the light of God's glory. He then gathered the Israelites together, reminded them of God's laws, and put them to work building God's tabernacle. With this, God's plans were in motion following the golden calf diversion.

H

E

A

R

43//EXODUS 40

MEMORY VERSES: EXODUS 33:16; MATTHEW 22:37-39

The Israelites assembled the tabernacle and all its components just as God instructed. It was a concerted effort on the part of Moses' leadership, the skill of numerous craftsmen, and the gifts of many people. After the tabernacle was constructed, Moses consecrated it and appointed Aaron and his sons as priests. Then, God's glory filled the tabernacle, an act showing His approval of their obedience and His presence among them. Additionally, the cloud of God's glory in the temple became the guide for the Israelites' journey. The people had come a long way from their time as slaves in Egypt, despite their repeated sin and disobedience along the way.

H

E

A

R

44//LEVITICUS 8–9

MEMORY VERSES: EXODUS 33:16; MATTHEW 22:37-39

The tabernacle was a place where God's presence could dwell among His people. For this reason, the people needed to know how to live properly in His presence, which is the purpose of the Book of Leviticus and the priesthood it describes. The role of a priest was one of a mediator between God and the people. God would speak to the people through the priests, and the priests would speak to God on behalf of the people. The priests also offered sacrifices to God on behalf of the people's sins. While the Levitical priests served God's purpose well during their time, they are a reminder for us that Jesus is the better priest, as Hebrews 7 describes. The Levitical priests were human. Therefore, each of them eventually died because of their sin. Their ability to atone for the people's sins was limited at best. As our great High Priest, however, Jesus is sinless and eternal, meaning His sacrifice is perfect and everlasting.

H

E

A

R

45//LEVITICUS 16–17

MEMORY VERSES: EXODUS 33:16; MATTHEW 22:37-39

One of the most important parts of the priests' job was overseeing the Day of Atonement. This day was set aside as the only day of the year when the high priest could enter the holy of holies and appear before the ark of the covenant. On the Day of Atonement, the high priest offered sacrifices to seek God's forgiveness for the sins of the people. From the beginning, God has made a way for His sinful people to remain in fellowship with Him, even though they can do nothing to deserve it. The Day of Atonement served this purpose until the crucifixion of Jesus, at which time animal sacrifices for sins were no longer required thanks to the bodily sacrifice of Jesus Himself. Today, God continues to draw His people back to Him when they sin through the conviction of the Holy Spirit. The Holy Spirit is the very presence of God living in every follower of Christ, and He guides us toward holiness and Christlikeness.

H

E

A

R

46//LEVITICUS 23

MEMORY VERSES: LEVITICUS 26:13; DEUTERONOMY 31:7-8

Part of God's plans for His covenant people included several festivals and holidays that served as a time for the people to gather together and worship God. All of the instructions God laid out for His people in Leviticus were intentional, and each of these festivals had important significance for their relationship with God. The Sabbath, which occurred weekly, was a day of rest and reflection meant to refocus the people's attention on God. The festivals celebrated God's redemption of His people from Egypt and His provisions for their physical and spiritual needs. The Day of Atonement constituted a day of self-denial in which the Israelites confessed their sins and the high priest made an atonement sacrifice. These special periods would also help the people remember God's acts of creation, deliverance, protection, and provision.

As you read the Bible this week...

H I G H L I G H T the verses that speak to you.

Write out the name of the book:

Which chapter and verse numbers stand out to you?

E X P L A I N what this passage means.

To whom was it originally written? Why?

How does it fit with the verses before and after it?

What is the Holy Spirit intending to communicate through this text?

A P P L Y what God is saying in these verses to your life.

What does this mean today?

What is God saying to you personally?

How can you apply this message to your life?

R E S P O N D to what you've read.

In what ways does this passage call you to action?

How will you be different because of what you've learned?

Write out a prayer to God in response to what you read today:

47//LEVITICUS 26

MEMORY VERSES: LEVITICUS 26:13; DEUTERONOMY 31:7-8

God reminded His people not to worship idols and to honor the Sabbath. He declared that obedience to His commands would bring blessing and life, while disobedience would bring curse and difficulty. If, after disobeying, His people repented and sought His forgiveness, they could again experience blessing and life. This cyclical pattern of obedience, blessing, disobedience, cursing, and redemption is the running theme throughout all of the Old Testament, and it's not until Jesus comes that the pattern is finally broken. God's favor is not dependent on our obedience. Because of Jesus' obedience, faith in Him is all that is necessary to have a relationship with God.

H

E

A

R

48//NUMBERS 11–12

MEMORY VERSES: LEVITICUS 26:13; DEUTERONOMY 31:7-8

The Book of Numbers picks up with the story of the Israelites' journey from Egypt to the promised land where it left off in the Book of Exodus. After the people built the tabernacle, they resumed their journey to the promised land, but their lack of faith in God again became evident when they complained about their condition. The complaints stirred up God's anger, but Moses interceded on behalf of the people and God held back His anger. This unique relationship Moses had with God stirred up jealousy in his brother, Aaron, and his sister, Miriam. When Miriam criticized Moses' marriage and questioned his leadership, God struck her with leprosy, banishing her from the camp. However, Moses again interceded to God for her healing. Both of these accounts remind us of the human bent toward sinfulness and our need for an intercessor, which we have in Jesus.

H

E

A

R

49//NUMBERS 13–14

MEMORY VERSES: LEVITICUS 26:13; DEUTERONOMY 31:7-8

The Israelites sent 12 scouts into Canaan, the promised land, in preparation for invasion. Although God had commanded the people to enter the land, ten of the spies returned with a negative report and warned the people not to enter because of the size and strength of the inhabitants. Only Joshua and Caleb urged the people to overcome their fears and to obey God's command to enter. As a result of the negative report, God punished the nation by declaring they would not be allowed to enter Canaan. One of the character traits of God made evident throughout the Old Testament is His justice, which is on display in this tragic scene. Because God is just, He could not allow a rebellious people to claim His blessing. Thankfully, faith in Jesus alone is enough to satisfy God's just wrath against our sin, but God still expects obedience from His people. We are able to obey Him through the power of His Holy Spirit. Growing in obedience and trust is the focus of the Christian life.

H

E

A

R

50//NUMBERS 16–17

MEMORY VERSES: LEVITICUS 26:13; DEUTERONOMY 31:7-8

As punishment for their disobedience, the Israelites would wander in the desert for 40 years, and most would die there, never seeing the promised land. During their wandering years, the Israelites' rebellion against God grew. Numbers 16–17 describe a rebellion that stirred up against Moses and Aaron's leadership, led by a Levite named Korah. The rebellion was stopped when God supernaturally destroyed the opponents and sent a plague among the Israelites as divine punishment. God then demonstrated His choice of Aaron and his descendants as priests. One of the most dangerous threats to a person's relationship with God is control, or self-sufficiency. This dangerous thought causes us to think we know what is better for our lives and how to achieve it. Until we surrender complete control to God, we are unable to walk in the freedom and peace He offers.

H

E

A

R

51//NUMBERS 20; 27:12-23

MEMORY VERSES: DEUTERONOMY 4:7; DEUTERONOMY 6:4-9

This point in Israel's story marks 40 years since they escaped from Egypt. Most of the people died in the desert and never stepped into the promised land because of their disobedience. A new generation would soon enter the promised land. Unfortunately, this generation continued their parents' pattern of rebellion against God for the lack of water at Kadesh. God instructed Moses to speak to the rock to bring water from it, but the people's grumbling drove him to strike the rock in impatience. Moses and Aaron failed to obey the Lord's instructions, thereby missing an opportunity to demonstrate their faith in God before the people. This failure, along with a rebellious attitude against God's people, resulted in Moses being disqualified from entering the promised land. This account is a tragic realization that all of us are susceptible to sin. Numbers 27 reveals that Joshua was commissioned to succeed Moses and lead Israel into Canaan.

As you read the Bible this week...

H IGHLIGHT the verses that speak to you.

Write out the name of the book:

Which chapter and verse numbers stand out to you?

E XPLAIN what this passage means.

To whom was it originally written? Why?

How does it fit with the verses before and after it?

What is the Holy Spirit intending to communicate through this text?

A PPLY what God is saying in these verses to your life.

What does this mean today?

What is God saying to you personally?

How can you apply this message to your life?

R ESPOND to what you've read.

In what ways does this passage call you to action?

How will you be different because of what you've learned?

Write out a prayer to God in response to what you read today:

52//NUMBERS 34–35

MEMORY VERSES: DEUTERONOMY 4:7; DEUTERONOMY 6:4-9

The time for God's people to enter the promised land had come, just as God had promised to Abraham, Isaac, and Jacob. God outlined in great detail how the land would be divided among the 12 tribes of Israel. God intentionally dispersed the Levites among all of the territories to serve as a reminder of their need for holiness, righteousness, and obedience. God also designated cities of refuge across the land as a place of escape and protection for a person who unintentionally murdered another person. The cities of refuge were more than just a place of retreat; they were a reminder of God's faithfulness to His people. Even today, God invites all of us, no matter what we have done, to take refuge in Him made possible by Jesus' life, death, and resurrection.

H

E

A

R

53//DEUTERONOMY 1–2

MEMORY VERSES: DEUTERONOMY 4:7; DEUTERONOMY 6:4-9

At the beginning of the Israelites' journey to the promised land, God made a covenant with Moses that included the giving of the Law. By the time the people reached the promised land, almost 40 years had passed. Most of the original generation that left Egypt had died. Before the people inhabited the land, God reminded them of His expectations. In summary, this is the purpose of the Book of Deuteronomy, which in large part is the record of Moses' speech to the people. Moses began his speech with a reminder to the people of what had taken place since leaving Egypt. Moses reiterated God's faithfulness. He desired for them to learn from the mistakes of their ancestors. Both Scripture and our relationships with other believers serve a similar purpose in our lives today. As we look back on how God has been faithful to His people throughout history, our own faith and trust in Him is strengthened.

H

E

A

R

54//DEUTERONOMY 3–4

MEMORY VERSES: DEUTERONOMY 4:7; DEUTERONOMY 6:4-9

In addition to reminding the Israelites of God's providence over their lives, Moses offered detailed instructions on how they were to live moving forward. What mattered most was that they remain faithful to God through obedience to His commands. Moses warned the people of the temptations idolatry presented. He encouraged them to teach each generation to obey the Lord. Keeping God's laws was essential to the people's prosperity and security. God promised that their wholehearted, consistent obedience would result in long lives in the land. Alternately, if they disobeyed they would experience the curses of divine discipline. Even today, we demonstrate our love for God by obeying His ways, teaching younger generations about Him, and declaring the truths of His Word to the world.

H

E

A

R

55//DEUTERONOMY 6–7

MEMORY VERSES: DEUTERONOMY 4:7; DEUTERONOMY 6:4-9

Deuteronomy 6 contains one of the most important passages in the Old Testament, the Shema (Deut. 6:4-9). These verses sum up what obedience to God looks like. Jesus referenced this text when He was asked what the greatest commandment was (Matt. 22:37-39). Moses instructed the people to love God with all their heart, soul, and strength. That single command encompassed all of the instructions of God. The idea was so important that they were told to teach their children this command, write it on door posts, and make signs. By God's grace, He had chosen the Israelites to be His people, and loving obedience was the only appropriate response to His grace. Today, God's chosen people are those who believe in His Son. Like the ancient Israelites, we are simply recipients of His grace, and He expects the same wholehearted love and obedience from us.

H

E

A

R

56//DEUTERONOMY 8–9

MEMORY VERSES: JOSHUA 1:8-9; PSALM 1:1-2

As Moses continued in his speech to the Israelites, he warned them of the temptation to forget about God and their need for Him. Moses knew, as is true for us also, that when things are going well in life, it's easy to forget about our total dependency on God. Remembering God's great acts of deliverance from the past would be a way to keep their need for Him at the forefront of their minds. Moses also reminded the Israelites that they were undeserving recipients of God's grace, and the golden calf episode was a glaring reminder of that truth. God's grace in their lives was based on His righteousness alone, as it is for God's children today. As the apostle Paul points out, "He made the One who did not know sin to be sin for us, so that we might become the righteousness of God in Him" (2 Cor. 5:21).

As you read the Bible this week...

HIGHLIGHT the verses that speak to you.

Write out the name of the book:

Which chapter and verse numbers stand out to you?

EXPLAIN what this passage means.

To whom was it originally written? Why?

How does it fit with the verses before and after it?

What is the Holy Spirit intending to communicate through this text?

APPLY what God is saying in these verses to your life.

What does this mean today?

What is God saying to you personally?

How can you apply this message to your life?

RESPOND to what you've read.

In what ways does this passage call you to action?

How will you be different because of what you've learned?

Write out a prayer to God in response to what you read today:

57//DEUTERONOMY 30–31

MEMORY VERSES: JOSHUA 1:8-9; PSALM 1:1-2

Deuteronomy 30 paints a vivid picture of God's mercy and grace against the rebellious heart of humanity—despite their patterns of rebellion. God promised to remain faithful to His covenant people. In Deuteronomy 30:11-20, Moses summarized the choice every person faces: the choice of life or death. Moses challenged the people to "choose life," that is, to choose for themselves the path of life and blessing instead of the path of selfishness that leads to death. With that reminder, Moses handed the torch of leadership over to Joshua. Even for believers who have God's promise of forgiveness and eternal life, walking with Christ involves a continual, conscious choice of right over wrong, faithful obedience over selfish disobedience. Like the Israelites, we are called to choose the path of life.

H

E

A

R

58//DEUTERONOMY 32:48-52; 34

MEMORY VERSES: JOSHUA 1:8-9; PSALM 1:1-2

The last chapters of Deuteronomy report Moses' final actions before passing the leadership baton to Joshua. Up to the very end of his life, Moses sought to live out the calling the Lord had given him at the burning bush. The Book of Deuteronomy ends with a description of Moses as a leader and prophet who had a relationship with God unlike any other. From the time of Moses, God's people looked forward to another Prophet who would come after Moses. Jesus Christ ultimately fulfilled that expectation. As Hebrews 3 tells us, Jesus is the true Savior who provided a way of redemption from sin, established the new covenant through His death on the cross for our sins, and thus had a greater glory than Moses.

H

E

A

R

59//JOSHUA 1–2

MEMORY VERSES: JOSHUA 1:8-9; PSALM 1:1-2

After Moses' death, God instructed Joshua to prepare the Israelites to enter the promised land. As Joshua faced the greatest challenge of his life, God reassured him of His continuing presence and challenged the new leader to show courage and to carefully follow God's instructions. In preparation for entering Canaan, Joshua sent two men to scout the city of Jericho. The men found refuge from Rahab, a prostitute whose house was located on the city wall. Rahab heard about the God of the Israelites and understood He was unique, and that motivated her to action. Before the Israelites even entered Canaan, God was making His glory known among the people there. Rahab not only expressed her faith in God verbally, but she acted in ways that demonstrated her faith in God was genuine. Hebrews 11:31 points to Rahab as an example of heroic faith.

H

E

A

R

60//JOSHUA 3–4

Joshua 3–4 describe the moment the Israelites had been waiting for since they crossed the Red Sea and escaped the Egyptians: finally crossing into the promised land. After a 40-year diversion because of their unfaithfulness, the time finally came. Just as God miraculously enabled them to cross the Red Sea, He again enabled them to cross the Jordan River on dry land. The two river crossings show God's consistent presence with and protection of His people. After they crossed, Joshua instructed one man from each tribe to gather a stone to build a memorial. That memorial served as a reminder of God's faithfulness and power for the Israelites and future generations. God continues to work miracles in the lives of His children today, not the least of which is the gift of salvation that none of us deserve. Taking the time to reflect on God's gifts and miraculous works is a vital part of a relationship with Him.

H

_____

E

_____

_____

_____

A

_____

_____

_____

R

_____

_____

_____

_____

61//JOSHUA 5:10-15; 6

MEMORY VERSES: JOSHUA 24:14-15; JUDGES 2:12

After God led the Israelites across the Jordan, they found themselves in a position to claim the promised land through a series of military victories as they conquered Canaan's major cities. The first city to be attacked was Jericho, but before Joshua could formulate a plan, he received a visit from a heavenly messenger who gave him instructions on how to overtake it. Noticeably absent from the plan was military strategy; Jericho would be overtaken by trust and obedience alone. God was clearly in control. Joshua needed to display trust in God's plan by following His instructions. On the seventh day, the people marched around the city seven times, blew trumpets, and shouted. Then God delivered the city into the Israelites' hands, all except for Rahab and her family, whom He had promised to protect because she helped God's people. We must always remember that God keeps His promises. He is who He says He is and does what He says He will do.

As you read the Bible this week...

HIGHLIGHT the verses that speak to you.

Write out the name of the book:

Which chapter and verse numbers stand out to you?

EXPLAIN what this passage means.

To whom was it originally written? Why?

How does it fit with the verses before and after it?

What is the Holy Spirit intending to communicate through this text?

APPLY what God is saying in these verses to your life.

What does this mean today?

What is God saying to you personally?

How can you apply this message to your life?

RESPOND to what you've read.

In what ways does this passage call you to action?

How will you be different because of what you've learned?

Write out a prayer to God in response to what you read today:

62//JOSHUA 7–8

MEMORY VERSES: JOSHUA 24:14-15; JUDGES 2:12

One of the instructions God gave His people as they overtook Jericho was not to seize any wealth or treasures of the Canaanites. God orchestrated this conquest, and the goal was to bring glory to His name; a focus on material gain would distract the people from this goal. One man, Achan, violated God's instruction, and his greed had a devastating impact on him, his family, and the community as a whole. After this sin was brought to light and dealt with, Joshua was able to lead the people in a successful conquest of their next city, Ai. Joshua knew this takeover, like Jericho, only happened because God allowed it to, so he responded in worship and a renewal of the covenant with God. The opportunity God gave the Israelites for a second chance to conquer Ai, despite Achan's disobedience, is a reminder for us of God's grace and willingness to restore those He loves. When we address our sins through confession and repentance, God is quick to forgive us and restore us to a right relationship with Him.

H

E

A

R

63//JOSHUA 23–24

MEMORY VERSES: JOSHUA 24:14-15; JUDGES 2:12

Chapters 9–22 of Joshua describe the Israelites' conquering the promised land and settling there. The book ends with Joshua's farewell address to the people, in which he reminded them of God's power and faithfulness to His promises and their need to be strong in faith, obedient to the covenant, and loyal to God. Joshua recapped how God had proven Himself faithful to them and His covenant from as far back as the time of Abraham. Joshua's address closed with a challenge to the people to renew their commitment to and worship of God alone, and the people accepted. Like the Israelites, we live in a world with many influences that can distract us from complete devotion to Christ. Joshua's challenge reminds us that if we hope to devote our lives exclusively to the Lord, we must hear and obey the Word of God and renew our commitment to Him every day.

H

E

A

R

64//JUDGES 2–3

MEMORY VERSES: JOSHUA 24:14-15; JUDGES 2:12

The Book of Judges continues the story of Israel's efforts to take control of the promised land following the death of their leader, Joshua. It becomes evident that the nation started to drift astray despite the commitment to God they had made before Joshua's death. Judges 2:10 reveals the shocking truth that a new generation of Israelites arose who did not know God and did not remember His works among their people. This new generation disobeyed God and abandoned the covenant of their fathers. In turn, God's judgment came down on them through military defeats and oppression by other nations. After this oppression had gone on for several years, the people finally called out to God for mercy, and God responded by delivering them through Othniel, the first of His appointed judges—the new form of leadership God put in place. This pattern of sin, oppression, repentance, and deliverance through a new judge continues throughout the book, and it paints a clear picture of humanity's bent toward sin and God's inexhaustible love.

H

E

A

R

65//JUDGES 4

MEMORY VERSES: JOSHUA 24:14-15; JUDGES 2:12

When the Israelites again turned to evil, God allowed them to be oppressed by a Canaanite king for 20 years, at which point they finally cried out for deliverance again. God heard their cries, and He responded by appointing Deborah as their new judge. In addition to being a judge, Deborah was also a prophet who delivered God's messages to the Israelites. She served as God's spiritual spokesperson to Barak, who was Israel's military leader. God used the joint efforts of Deborah and Barak to defeat the Canaanite forces that oppressed His people. Deborah stands out as one of the godly leaders in Israel's history. She listened and obeyed the words of God, had faith in His ability to work through her, and encouraged the ways God was working in other people. Deborah also modeled what Jesus would later confirm—we demonstrate our love for God and obedience to Him through a life of service to others.

H

E

A

R

66//JUDGES 6–7

MEMORY VERSES: PSALM 19:14; GALATIANS 4:4-5

After 40 years of peace, the Israelites again fell into idol worship, and God allowed them to suffer oppression for seven years. When they cried out for help, God called a young farmer named Gideon to deliver them. The first thing revealed about Gideon was his fear, something that would plague him throughout his leadership. In fear, Gideon requested two signs of assurance that he truly was speaking with God, which God supplied. The great test of Gideon's leadership came when God called him into battle against the Midianites, then reduced the army to just a few hundred men. As God had done in the battle of Jericho, He reminded the people that His presence was all they needed. We do not need signs from God to know that He continues to faithfully deliver His people from sin. God made His role as Deliverer clear when He sent His own Son to the cross to deliver His people from sin and death once and for all.

As you read the Bible this week...

HIGHLIGHT the verses that speak to you.

Write out the name of the book:

Which chapter and verse numbers stand out to you?

EXPLAIN what this passage means.

To whom was it originally written? Why?

How does it fit with the verses before and after it?

What is the Holy Spirit intending to communicate through this text?

APPLY what God is saying in these verses to your life.

What does this mean today?

What is God saying to you personally?

How can you apply this message to your life?

RESPOND to what you've read.

In what ways does this passage call you to action?

How will you be different because of what you've learned?

Write out a prayer to God in response to what you read today:

67//JUDGES 13–14

Another spiritual regression by the Israelites brought yet another judge onto the scene—Samson. To set Samson apart for God's work, he was bound by the Nazirite vow even before his birth, which meant he couldn't cut his hair, touch a corpse or carcass of a dead animal, or consume alcohol. Furthermore, the Spirit of God gave Samson extraordinary strength. Unfortunately, as chapter 14 reveals, Samson failed to remember and keep God's commands; instead, he gave in to the passions and lusts of the world and married a Philistine woman, something specifically outlawed by God. Early on, we see hints that pride and self-indulgence would be Samson's downfalls. Samson's story reminds us that humility is one of the most important virtues in the kingdom of God. With a healthy, balanced view of ourselves in relation to God, we put ourselves in a position to be used by God and to reflect His humility and love to the world.

H

E

A

R

68//JUDGES 15–16

MEMORY VERSES: PSALM 19:14; GALATIANS 4:4-5

During a time of separation from his wife, Samson discovered that her father had given her in marriage to another man. Exacting revenge, Samson killed 1,000 Philistine men with the jawbone of a donkey. Later, Samson fell in love with a woman named Delilah whom Philistine leaders bribed to uncover the secret of Samson's strength so they could capture, humiliate, and kill him. When Delilah shaved off Samson's braids, the Spirit left him and he lost the true source of his strength—God Himself. Samson was then captured and blinded by the Philistines. Still hoping to conquer the Philistines, Samson prayed to the Lord for strength, and his prayer was answered. While God was dishonored by Samson's sinful behavior, God nevertheless honored the calling He had given Samson. God is always faithful to the calling and gifts with which He equips us to serve Him. He responds faithfully to our faith, however weak and confused we may be: "If we are faithless, He remains faithful, for He cannot deny Himself" (2 Tim. 2:13).

H

E

A

R

69//RUTH 1–2

MEMORY VERSES: PSALM 19:14; GALATIANS 4:4-5

During the time of the judges, a severe famine broke out in Israel, so an Israelite man named Elimelech moved with his wife, Naomi, and two sons from Bethlehem in Judah to the land of Moab. While there, Elimelech died, both sons married Moabite women, and then both sons also died. Naomi decided to return to her home in Judah, and her daughter-in-law Ruth chose to go with her, a choice that revealed her love, her loyalty, and her undying commitment to Naomi. Ruth even went so far as to pledge allegiance to Naomi's God. Once in Bethlehem, Ruth took the initiative to help provide for Naomi by gleaning in the nearby grain fields. In the process, Ruth was noticed and befriended by a man named Boaz, one of Naomi's relatives who provided the two widows with grain and protection in a generous display of kindness. The story of Ruth is the story of God's providential love on display—a love that extends to all people who have faith in Him.

H

E

A

R

70//RUTH 3–4

MEMORY VERSES: PSALM 19:14; GALATIANS 4:4-5

Boaz's commitment to Ruth and Naomi unfolds in Ruth 3–4. With Naomi's guidance, Ruth approached Boaz and asked him to be her family redeemer—a relative who took on the responsibility of caring for a woman after her husband died. Without a redeemer, the widow would be left destitute in a society that did not make it easy on widows to prosper. In response to Ruth's request, Boaz followed the process for becoming her redeemer, and the two eventually married. By giving Ruth a husband and a son, the Lord graciously redeemed Ruth's seemingly hopeless situation. The story of Ruth and Boaz reminds us of the gospel, when Jesus Christ came to earth to be our Redeemer. We were born into the hopelessness of sin, but through the death and resurrection of Jesus, God redeems us, He buys us back into His family, and He secures our eternal future with Him.

H

E

A

R

71//1 SAMUEL 1–2

MEMORY VERSES: 1 SAMUEL 15:22; 1 SAMUEL 16:7

During the time of the judges, Israel reached a spiritual low point. The priesthood was corrupt, as the behavior of Eli's sons reveals, and many people turned away from the faith of their forefathers. However, from the beginning of 1 Samuel, it becomes evident that a remnant of faithful Israelites still remained. First Samuel 1–2 describes the fervent prayers of Hannah, a faithful woman who was desperate for a child. Hannah pleaded with God to give her a son whom, in return, she would give back to God in commitment to His service. God answered Hannah's prayer. She gave birth to Samuel, who was dedicated to God for a lifetime of service as she promised. Samuel was the last judge of Israel, and to this day his mother is an example of the self-sacrificial nature God expects from His children.

As you read the Bible this week...

HIGHLIGHT the verses that speak to you.

Write out the name of the book:

Which chapter and verse numbers stand out to you?

EXPLAIN what this passage means.

To whom was it originally written? Why?

How does it fit with the verses before and after it?

What is the Holy Spirit intending to communicate through this text?

APPLY what God is saying in these verses to your life.

What does this mean today?

What is God saying to you personally?

How can you apply this message to your life?

RESPOND to what you've read.

In what ways does this passage call you to action?

How will you be different because of what you've learned?

Write out a prayer to God in response to what you read today:

72//1 SAMUEL 3; 8

From the time he was a little boy, Samuel served as an apprentice to Eli, the priest. During this time, God called Samuel to a life of prophetic ministry. While resting near the ark, Samuel heard the Lord speak to him. God took the initiative, as He always does, and after some confusion about whose voice he heard, Samuel submitted to God. Without yet knowing what God was specifically asking, Samuel enlisted himself into service. Over the years, Samuel continued to grow in his relationship with God and in his responsibilities to the nation during a transitional and unstable time in their history. The people voiced their desire to be more like their neighboring nations, who were all ruled by kings, and they hoped that becoming a monarchy would give them strength against their enemies. So they asked Samuel to appoint a king to govern them—a request that flew in the face of their identity as God's chosen people, set apart from all other nations. God granted their request, but considered it simply another of the many rebellious choices of Israel.

H

E

A

R

73//1 SAMUEL 9–10

MEMORY VERSES: 1 SAMUEL 15:22; 1 SAMUEL 16:7

The Israelites rebelled against God by demanding a king, and Samuel, with God's approval, granted their request. Even though a monarchy was not God's desire for the people, God still took it upon Himself to select who would be the nation's first king. God worked through a series of seemingly unrelated events to reveal who that king would be. Saul, in the process of searching for some lost donkeys, solicited the help of Samuel. All of this happened according to God's predicted plan, which revealed to Samuel that Saul was God's appointed leader. From the beginning of Saul's story, though, we see hints of the life-long struggle that would plague his leadership—a lack of trust in God (9:21; 10:22). Saul's life is a sad story of unrealized potential, but it's an important reminder of God's desire that we trust Him and His plans for our lives, resulting in our unwavering devotion.

H

E

A

R

74//1 SAMUEL 13–14

MEMORY VERSES: 1 SAMUEL 15:22; 1 SAMUEL 16:7

One of the consequences of Israel's new monarchy was a renewed conflict with the Philistines, Israel's enemy neighbor. Saul experienced military victory, which encouraged the people in their ability to fight back against the Philistines. First Samuel 13–14 draw a comparison between the leadership of Saul and Jonathan, Saul's son and commander of half of Israel's army. Saul was consumed by his own selfish goals, to the point that he ignored God's instruction and usurped the role of priest, offering a sacrifice that displeased God. This pattern of disobedience would lead to an abrupt end to Saul's reign, when he would be replaced by David, "a man after [God's] own heart" (13:14, ESV). Jonathan, on the other hand, acknowledged trust in God's power and leadership, seeking confirmation from God before acting. The lives of these two men are a reminder that what you believe about God determines the actions you take in your relationship with Him.

H

E

A

R

75//1 SAMUEL 15–16

MEMORY VERSES: 1 SAMUEL 15:22; 1 SAMUEL 16:7

Saul's repeated disobedience had disastrous consequences for him and his family. God equated Saul's failure to obey with idolatry, and for that, he would remove him as king. This set the stage for David, who would go down in history as Israel's greatest king. In 1 Samuel 13:14, Samuel described the next king as a man after God's own heart, but very little else is told about David other than his unassuming build and his work as a shepherd. That didn't matter, though, because God chose him to be king and anointed him with His Holy Spirit, and those were the only qualifications that mattered. The same is true of God's people today—God has chosen you to serve Him, and He has equipped you for that task by giving you the presence of His very Spirit. Like David, the Holy Spirit is committed to making you into a person after God's own heart, and all you have to do is surrender in order to allow Him to do so.

H

E

A

R

76//1 SAMUEL 17–18

MEMORY VERSES: 1 SAMUEL 17:46-47; 2 TIMOTHY 4:17A

The story of David and Goliath is one of the most well-known in Scripture. The Philistine army challenged the Israelite army to a battle between their greatest champions. The Philistine champion was the giant Goliath, whose presence was so foreboding no Israelite wanted the seemingly impossible challenge of battling him. David (who was simply delivering lunch to his older brothers in the army) was offended by the mockery Goliath hurled against Israel's God, so he used his slingshot and the power of God Himself to kill the giant. Chapter 18 tells how, in the aftermath of his victory over Goliath, David's life changed both for the better and the worse—he discovered a lasting friend in Jonathan and a bitter rival in Saul. David's defeat of Goliath is a great biblical account, but it's also a picture of the gospel. In Christ, we have an even greater King than David—a King who defeated the giants of sin and death to set His people free.

As you read the Bible this week...

H I G H L I G H T the verses that speak to you.

Write out the name of the book:

Which chapter and verse numbers stand out to you?

E X P L A I N what this passage means.

To whom was it originally written? Why?

How does it fit with the verses before and after it?

What is the Holy Spirit intending to communicate through this text?

A P P L Y what God is saying in these verses to your life.

What does this mean today?

What is God saying to you personally?

How can you apply this message to your life?

R E S P O N D to what you've read.

In what ways does this passage call you to action?

How will you be different because of what you've learned?

Write out a prayer to God in response to what you read today:

77//1 SAMUEL 19–20

MEMORY VERSES: 1 SAMUEL 17:46-47; 2 TIMOTHY 4:17A

Saul's jealousy of David's accomplishments drove him mad, so he ordered David's death. However, Jonathan warned David and he escaped. Once again, Jonathan stands out as a model for believers today. Jonathan understood that God had appointed David to be the next king, and he knew his father's actions did not bring honor to God. Even though Saul was Jonathan's father, Jonathan was submissive first and foremost to the Lord. No one had a greater claim on Jonathan's life than God. David and Jonathan solidified their friendship with a covenant of loyalty to one another and to God. As Jesus teaches in the Great Commandment, loyalty and submission to God are to take first priority in the life of a Christian, but this also naturally encompasses loving others, as Jonathan modeled so well.

H

E

A

R

78//1 SAMUEL 21–22

MEMORY VERSES: 1 SAMUEL 17:46-47; 2 TIMOTHY 4:17A

Although parts of David's life give a clear foreshadowing of Christ, it doesn't take long for us to be reminded that David was still human. David fled into exile because Saul wanted to kill him, and during that time he made a series of selfish decisions that revealed his lack of faith that God would protect him and bring him into power as He had promised. While David may not have thought much about his actions, they had a devastating impact on Ahimelech and 85 other priests who were all murdered by Saul for the role Ahimelech played in assisting David. But one of the things that makes David a hero of our faith is his example of repentance. When David learned of these deaths, he acknowledged his sin and attempted to make it right. Throughout his life, David would sin many times, sometimes with tragic consequences, but he always repented and returned to the Lord. Even more importantly, God always accepted him back and continued to use David to make His name known. Like David, we sin often, but God is quick to forgive us and shower us with His grace when we repent of our sins and return to Him.

H

E

A

R

79//PSALM 22; 1 SAMUEL 24–25:1

MEMORY VERSES: 1 SAMUEL 17:46-47; 2 TIMOTHY 4:17A

During his life, David penned many of the psalms that are now included in the Bible. Psalm 22 came from a time in David's life when he found himself in great despair. David knew the plans God had for his life, but at that moment they felt unattainable and God felt absent. However, by the end of his prayer, David's pleas turned to praise and he acknowledged that although God felt far away, David knew He was not. While we don't know from what specific circumstances this psalm stemmed, David's experience in 1 Samuel 24 parallels it well. Saul's pursuit of David forced him to hide in a cave, an isolated place where he undoubtedly felt helpless. But when presented with the opportunity to kill Saul, David did not. In that moment, David chose to claim God's promises for his life and his future and to trust God to bring them to fruition. This is the same example Jesus gave us on the cross when He echoed David's cry—"My God, My God, why have you forsaken Me?"—but even so, both Jesus and David surrendered their very lives to the plans of their Father.

H

E

A

R

80//1 SAMUEL 28; 31

MEMORY VERSES: 1 SAMUEL 17:46-47; 2 TIMOTHY 4:17A

These final chapters of Saul's story tell a tragic end to his life and reveal the consequences of his failure to trust God, just as his early years foreshadowed. After years of Saul failing to listen to God, God finally quit speaking to him. When confronted with a new threat from the Philistines, Saul approached a medium—a witch—in hopes that she could speak with Samuel's spirit and get him the spiritual wisdom he needed for this battle. This act was done in direct disobedience to the laws of God—laws Saul had previously sought to uphold by banning the practice of mediums altogether. Through the power of God, Samuel did speak to Saul, and his words summarized Saul's great failure in life—"You did not obey the Lord." Samuel then predicted what chapter 31 proved to be true: the Philistines would defeat the Israelites, and Saul and his sons would die in the battle. What Samuel didn't reveal, though, is that Saul would take his own life. From beginning to end, Saul's life shows us the missed opportunities and spiritual unrest of a person who refuses to live in submission to God.

H

E

A

R

81//2 SAMUEL 1; 2:1-7

MEMORY VERSES: PSALM 23:1-3; PSALM 51:10-13

In 1 Samuel 16, God chose David to replace Saul as king. After years of tension, wars, Saul's downfall, and David's patience, the time for David to take over the throne finally arrived. However, that time in David's life was not particularly joyful, for it was marked with grief over the deaths of Saul and Jonathan. David sang a lament to express his sadness, and that same lament became part of the nation's collective grieving for the loss of their king. David's lament marks a transition in the narrative from Saul's life to David's, which remains the focus for the rest of 2 Samuel. When the time of mourning for Saul and Jonathan was over, David asked the Lord to show him what to do next—a question that revealed his reliance upon God and his desire to live out his calling as God's anointed ruler. There is no question that David would be a much different king than Saul was and that David is the one whose obedience we should seek to emulate.

As you read the Bible this week...

H I G H L I G H T the verses that speak to you.

Write out the name of the book:

Which chapter and verse numbers stand out to you?

E X P L A I N what this passage means.

To whom was it originally written? Why?

How does it fit with the verses before and after it?

What is the Holy Spirit intending to communicate through this text?

A P P L Y what God is saying in these verses to your life.

What does this mean today?

What is God saying to you personally?

How can you apply this message to your life?

R E S P O N D to what you've read.

In what ways does this passage call you to action?

How will you be different because of what you've learned?

Write out a prayer to God in response to what you read today:

82//2 SAMUEL 3:1; 5; PSALM 23

MEMORY VERSES: PSALM 23:1-3; PSALM 51:10-13

David's rise to power was not without conflict between those loyal to him and those who were still loyal to Saul, but David was God's chosen leader. Soon after he became king, David attacked the Jebusites, a clan of the Canaanites, which marked a continuation of God's covenant instructions to take control of the promised land. David took control of the city of Jerusalem, but another war with the Philistines soon followed. Before responding to the Philistine threat, David sought God's guidance, which led to another victory. David realized that the source of His success was the Lord. God had been preparing David through both favorable and difficult circumstances to be the king of Israel, and His concern for His people was evident through David's actions. Second Samuel 5:10 notes an important truth that weaved throughout David's life: "David became more and more powerful, for the Lord God of Hosts, was with him." David recognized that God's presence and power were at the root of his success. No matter what David went through, he acknowledged that God was his Shepherd who would always be by his side. As David reminds us, God has promised to do whatever it takes to lead, guide, and protect us, and the very cross of Christ assures us that He will do just that.

H

E

A

R

83//2 SAMUEL 6–7

As one of his first actions after acquiring Jerusalem and making it his capital, David moved the ark of the covenant to the city. God's laws contained specific instructions for carrying the Ark, but the men moving it failed to follow all of the instructions, and one man died as a result. The setback caused David to reconsider his plans, and also opened his eyes to the holiness of God. After a three-month delay, he finally completed moving the ark to Jerusalem. Next, David planned a temple to house the ark, but God stopped him in the process. Even though David's motive was good, his desire was not in line with God's purpose or timetable. Construction on the temple would have to wait another generation. God did, however, make an eternal covenant with David that promised his kingdom would endure forever. The New Testament writers help us understand that the promises of the covenant with David were ultimately fulfilled in Jesus Christ, our eternal King (Acts 2:22-36).

H

E

A

R

84//PSALM 18; 2 SAMUEL 9

MEMORY VERSES: PSALM 23:1-3; PSALM 51:10-13

One of the highlights of David's friendship with Jonathan was the time when Jonathan helped protect David from Saul's wrath. In response, David made a promise with Jonathan to always show kindness to Jonathan's descendants. Now, as king, David had the chance to make good on that promise by giving Mephibosheth—Jonathan's crippled son—all of Saul's remaining property, inviting him to live under the protection of the palace. Jonathan had shown grace to David, so David extended that same grace to Mephibosheth. David's understanding of the character of God, as described in Psalm 18, motivated the love and grace he showed Mephibosheth. This story from David's time as king gives us an incredible illustration of the gospel in action. God has extended His grace to us by inviting us into His family through the salvation available in Christ. Once we accept God's gift of grace and become His children, He expects us to reflect His love and grace to the world in return.

H

E

A

R

85//2 SAMUEL 11–12

MEMORY VERSES: PSALM 23:1-3; PSALM 51:10-13

Second Samuel 11–12 tells the infamous account of David's adultery with Bathsheba, as well as the sinful actions and devastating consequences that followed. While David was God's anointed king whom God described as a man after His own heart, he was still very human with fully human temptations and desires. David had an affair with Bathsheba, a woman who was married to a man in David's army. The affair led to a pregnancy, which David attempted to cover up. When the cover-up didn't go as David planned, David had Bathsheba's husband murdered in battle, which highlights the destructive pattern of sin David was trapped in. David tried to keep his sin a secret, but God used the prophet Nathan to expose David's sin and move him toward confession and repentance. This story highlights the devastating consequences of sin in our lives and our relationships, but it also reveals the great lengths God goes to in order to bring us back to Him. Ultimately, this story is a reminder that while David was a great king, Jesus is the true and better King whose sinless, perfect life makes our own victory over sin possible.

H

E

A

R

86//PSALM 51

MEMORY VERSES: PSALM 1:1-6; PSALM 119:9-11

David wrote Psalm 51 after the prophet Nathan confronted him about his sins with Bathsheba and toward Uriah (2 Sam. 11–12). This psalm records David's cry to God for forgiveness, including his confession of sin, his plea for God's cleansing, his acknowledgment of God's holiness, and his request that God restore joy to David's life and blessing to Jerusalem. This psalm is an example for us of genuine sorrow over sin and the kind of repentant heart God desires. David's life reminds us that God is ready and willing to forgive repentant sinners completely and restore them to fellowship with Him. What matters to God is a truly "broken and humbled heart" (51:17). This attitude toward sin ushers in God's grace and forgiveness.

As you read the Bible this week...

H I G H L I G H T the verses that speak to you.

Write out the name of the book:

Which chapter and verse numbers stand out to you?

E X P L A I N what this passage means.

To whom was it originally written? Why?

How does it fit with the verses before and after it?

What is the Holy Spirit intending to communicate through this text?

A P P L Y what God is saying in these verses to your life.

What does this mean today?

What is God saying to you personally?

How can you apply this message to your life?

R E S P O N D to what you've read.

In what ways does this passage call you to action?

How will you be different because of what you've learned?

Write out a prayer to God in response to what you read today:

87//2 SAMUEL 24; PSALM 24

MEMORY VERSES: PSALM 1:1-6; PSALM 119:9-11

The last chapter of 2 Samuel continues the theme of God's blessing on David's life and the nation of Israel because of His faithfulness to His covenant. However, the events in this chapter are another example of God temporarily removing His blessing because of sin. The military census David took angered God because it happened at a time when the nation of Israel was at peace, which revealed David's interest in his own power and military success over his trust in the Lord. God responded to David's sin by punishing all of Israel, which opened David's eyes to the error of his ways and led to his confession of sin and repentance. Throughout David's life, we notice a cycle in his relationship with God that makes it look a lot like ours. David moved from a place of worship to sin, then to repentance, then back to worship. Second Samuel ends with David's example of costly sacrifice as a display of his worship toward God. This theme is the heart of Psalm 24, a psalm that acknowledges the power of God—the Author and Finisher of everything.

H

E

A

R

88//PSALMS 1; 19

MEMORY VERSES: PSALM 1:1-6; PSALM 119:9-11

From the beginning of time, God has been making Himself known. The two primary ways He reveals Himself are through creation and Scripture, both of which show God's power and glory. They come up repeatedly in the psalms, which the people of God used and still use to worship Him. Psalm 1 sets the course for the book by presenting an important teaching for life in general: Every person must choose the path he or she will follow—either the path of God or the path of self. One leads to abundant life, the other to destruction. The obvious correct choice is to choose the path of God, which means turning from sin and filling your life with Him and His Word. Psalm 19 echoes the benefit of choosing the right path and responding positively to God's revelation of Himself in creation and His Word. God's ultimate revelation of Himself, which all of Scripture points to, came in Jesus Christ, our Rock and our Redeemer (19:14). When we choose to live in obedience to God and His Word, we are choosing abundant life with Christ.

H

E

A

R

89//PSALMS 103; 119:1-48

MEMORY VERSES: PSALM 1:1-6; PSALM 119:9-11

In Psalm 103, David praised God because of all the good things He had done, outlining the benefits we receive from Him through His unmerited grace. David noted that the faithful love of God is great and incomparable. God is the ultimate Father in His compassion to His children, and for this He is worthy of our never-ending praise. Psalm 119 picks up some of the same themes from yesterday's readings in Psalms 1 and 19, as the psalmist praised God for His Word and the impact it had on his life. The God who forgives our sins, redeems our lives, and satisfies our desires (103:1-5) is the same God who gives us access into the very heart of who He is through His Word. Because God's Word is such a gift, He expects it to be taken seriously, which means we obey God's laws and look to His Word as the guide for our lives. The power, inspiration, and truth of God's Word demand the careful study and dedicated application of it, the end result of which is unspeakable joy (119:23-24).

H

E

A

R

90//PSALM 119:49-128

MEMORY VERSES: PSALM 1:1-6; PSALM 119:9-11

Psalm 119 is the longest psalm and the longest chapter of the Bible, and almost every verse describes an aspect of God's Word. The verses from today's reading teach us many truths about God and how we are to relate to Him. For example, God's faithful love comes to those who trust Him and brings hope to the afflicted. Reading and studying God's Word is also how people come to know God more deeply. God's Word is certain and eternal, and all of Scripture reveals the character and glory of God. As we can see from this psalm, God expects His people to know, obey, and delight in His Word. Doing so reveals our faith in and love for Him, and it keeps us on the path toward holiness—a pursuit that will take a lifetime.

H

E

A

R

91//PSALMS 119:129-176; 139

MEMORY VERSES: PSALM 139:1-3; PSALM 139:15-16

The remainder of Psalm 119 continues the theme of delighting in God's Word. Today's reading reminds us that while God's principles are a joy to obey, many people do not follow them. This truth should be a source of sorrow for us as it was for the psalmist, and it should compel us to live on mission for the gospel. Verses 153-159 teach that the way God's people show their love for Him is through obedience to His Word, which challenges us to oppose sin and pursue Christlikeness. Among the promises God makes to His people is the promise that He will help us as we strive to live, study, and obey His Word (119:169-176). This is encouraging no matter where we are in our spiritual journey. The psalm ends with a reminder that the goal of delighting in God's Word is obedience while we wait for our promised eternal life with God to become reality.

As you read the Bible this week...

H IGHLIGHT the verses that speak to you.

Write out the name of the book:

Which chapter and verse numbers stand out to you?

E XPLAIN what this passage means.

To whom was it originally written? Why?

How does it fit with the verses before and after it?

What is the Holy Spirit intending to communicate through this text?

A PPLY what God is saying in these verses to your life.

What does this mean today?

What is God saying to you personally?

How can you apply this message to your life?

R ESPOND to what you've read.

In what ways does this passage call you to action?

How will you be different because of what you've learned?

Write out a prayer to God in response to what you read today:

92//PSALMS 148–150

The Book of Psalms includes 150 individual psalms with themes that range from praise to lament and from thanksgiving to songs of ascent (specific psalms used during times of Israelite feasts and religious pilgrimages). Regardless of their original purpose or their tone, all of the psalms are hymns of worship to God. The book ends with three psalms of praise. Psalm 148 praises God for His glory, made evident through His creation. The final verse of that psalm references a "horn" God raised up for His people, which is a reference to the honor God bestows on His people through His redemptive grace. While God did this time and again for His people in the Old Testament, the final and perfect act came when He sent His Son to be our Redeemer. In Psalm 149, the focus remains on praising God, but the emphasis shifts to His acts on behalf of His people—the ultimate one being salvation, both physical and spiritual—and the appropriate way we should respond to Him. Psalm 150 closes the book with shouts of praise and the call for everything that has breath to praise the Lord. These psalms are a great reminder to us that, regardless of our present circumstances, God is always worthy of our praise, and that is the very act for which we were created.

H

E

A

R

93//1 KINGS 2

MEMORY VERSES: PSALM 139:1-3; PSALM 139:15-16

The Book of 1 Kings picks up where 2 Samuel left off with the transition from David's kingship to that of his son Solomon. Solomon's rise to power wasn't without controversy—Adonijah, his older brother, saw himself as the rightful heir to the throne, and Solomon killed him in order to maintain peace and establish his authority as king. After David made Solomon king, and as David was about to die, he gave Solomon some parting wisdom. David told Solomon to make obedience to God his priority so that God would continue to be faithful to His covenant promises. Solomon's predecessors—Saul and David—had learned the hard way the importance of obedience to their covenant with God. Both men had made mistakes that Solomon could learn from, but as his story unfolds, it becomes evident that Solomon too was a broken human leader unable to faithfully uphold his covenant with God. Thankfully, as God's children today, we are recipients of God's covenant of grace, which means our relationship with God is based on Jesus' perfect obedience rather than our own efforts.

H

E

A

R

94//1 KINGS 3; 6

MEMORY VERSES: PSALM 139:1-3; PSALM 139:15-16

With the kingship secured, Solomon turned his attention to ruling Israel. Early on, God appeared to Solomon in a dream and gave him the opportunity to ask for anything. Solomon knew that the responsibility he had as God's anointed king would require great wisdom, so that is what he asked for. God granted his request and gave him riches and honor as well. The story in 1 Kings 3:16-28 shows God was faithful to give Solomon the wisdom he asked for. During David's time as king, he had asked God to let him build a temple for Him, but God told him that was not part of His plan for David's rule; instead, that became Solomon's primary task as God's anointed leader. In the midst of Solomon's great success and grand projects, God gave guidance on how to genuinely honor Him. The key to honoring the Lord does not lie primarily in outward expressions of devotion, but in learning and obeying His commands. The temple could crumble (and eventually did), but unselfish dedication and service to God bear fruits that last for eternity.

H

E

A

R

95//1 KINGS 8; 9:1-9

MEMORY VERSES: PSALM 139:1-3; PSALM 139:15-16

With the temple and Solomon's own palace complete, Solomon assembled the elders of Israel at Jerusalem. The priests and Levites brought the ark of the Lord and the sacred furnishings from the tabernacle and placed them in the temple. After the Lord's glory in the form of a cloud filled the temple, Solomon offered a prayer of dedication, thanking God for keeping His promise to David, asking God to fulfill the remaining promises He had made to David (2 Sam. 7:5-16), and asking God to hear and answer the Israelites when they prayed in times of need. Then God spoke to Solomon and emphasized the importance of obedience for Israel's continued blessing. The call to obedience surfaces time and again in Scripture, which points to its significance as one of the most important disciplines a follower of God can develop. As Christians today, obedience to God does not earn us salvation—that has been freely given to us through Jesus. Instead, obedience is our loving response to God for who He is and all He has done for us. It's also the primary way we display our devotion to God to a watching world.

H

E

A

R

96//PROVERBS 1–2

MEMORY VERSES: PROVERBS 1:7; PROVERBS 3:5-6

The Book of Proverbs and the Book of Ecclesiastes are a result of Solomon's prayer for wisdom. Proverbs contains some of the most practical advice in the entire Bible, and its wisdom covers everything from relationships to leadership, from how to spend money to how to spend time. Proverbs begins by stating that the purpose of the book is to provide wisdom and insight for how to live as a child of God. Next, chapters 1–2 describe why a person should desire wisdom and the benefits wisdom brings to a person's life. At its core, wisdom is the skill of living life according to God's ways, which Solomon summarized in Proverbs 1:7, "The fear of the Lord is the beginning of knowledge; fools despise wisdom and discipline." Fear of God speaks to the awe and wonder that results from understanding who God is and how entirely dependent we are on Him. This is the foundation on which everything else in our lives is built.

As you read the Bible this week...

HIGHLIGHT the verses that speak to you.

Write out the name of the book:

Which chapter and verse numbers stand out to you?

EXPLAIN what this passage means.

To whom was it originally written? Why?

How does it fit with the verses before and after it?

What is the Holy Spirit intending to communicate through this text?

APPLY what God is saying in these verses to your life.

What does this mean today?

What is God saying to you personally?

How can you apply this message to your life?

RESPOND to what you've read.

In what ways does this passage call you to action?

How will you be different because of what you've learned?

Write out a prayer to God in response to what you read today:

97//PROVERBS 3–4

MEMORY VERSES: PROVERBS 1:7; PROVERBS 3:5-6

Proverbs 3–4 continue Solomon's instructions to those in their youth. In these two chapters, as in other parts of Proverbs, wisdom is personified as a woman seeking others who will listen to her teachings. Whether or not a person listens determines the path of his or her life. Those who fail to heed her instructions will suffer devastating consequences, while those who pursue wisdom will receive many benefits, as these chapters describe. In chapter 4, Solomon roots his plea for wise living in his own upbringing and the tradition of the Israelites—David passed down the importance of wisdom to Solomon, and Solomon passed it on to his children through discipleship. Chapter 3 makes it clear that we gain wisdom through the study of God's Word. The Bible is God's revelation of Himself and His truth, and it teaches us how to live for God and share His love with the world. The close of chapter 3 points out an important teaching—one of the reasons we need wisdom for living is so that we know how to relate in godly love to the people in our lives.

H

E

A

R

98//PROVERBS 16–18

PROVERBS 1:7; PROVERBS 3:5-6

Proverbs 16–18 are part of a larger division of the Book of Proverbs that contains wisdom for everyday life. Three of the most well-known proverbs are found in these chapters: "Pride comes before destruction, and an arrogant spirit before a fall" (16:18); "The name of Yahweh is a strong tower; the righteous run to it and are protected" (18:10); and "A man with many friends may be harmed, but there is a friend who stays closer than a brother" (18:24). These three proverbs show the diversity of topics and teachings presented throughout this book. From these proverbs alone, we are reminded that pride is a destructive sin, God is our Protector, and everyone needs the support and love of trusted friends. What these and all other proverbs have in common is that they teach us how to put God's values into practice in our daily lives, which is something we will spend the rest of our lives learning how to do.

H

E

A

R

99//PROVERBS 31

Proverbs 31 is known for its description of biblical womanhood. But this final proverb is about much more than being a woman. Proverbs 31 closes the book with a picture of godly wisdom on display in family life. The virtuous wife and mother described here gives all people an example to follow. The main principles affirmed in this proverb are a person's trustworthiness, responsibility, and godliness—characteristics that can only be lived out if you are seeking God's wisdom for daily living. Verse 30 draws attention to the fear of the Lord as an admirable quality, which brings the Book of Proverbs full circle from where it began in 1:7. Worship of and respectful submission to the Lord's authority is the key to wisdom in every area of life.

H

E

A

R

100//1 KINGS 11–12

PROVERBS 1:7; PROVERBS 3:5-6

First Kings 11 marks a turning point for Solomon and the Kingdom of Israel. At this point in his life, Solomon had 700 wives and 300 concubines whom he allowed to practice pagan religions, even constructing places of worship for them. Solomon's life of excessive wisdom and riches (which were originally gifts from God) led him to compromise his faith and his leadership through disobedience, and the consequences were quick and devastating. God judged Solomon by dividing the kingdom of Israel. Tensions had been growing among the tribes, and only the grace of God held the kingdom together. Now that it was no more, the kingdom of God's people divided into two. Although Solomon was a wise and godly ruler for much of his life, the end of his reign is yet another reminder of our need for a true and better King, which we have in Jesus. We are also reminded through this story of God's faithfulness to His people—God did not turn His back on either of the kingdoms, and the story of His faithfulness and pursuit of His people continued on toward completion.

H

E

A

R

101//1 KINGS 16:29-34; 17

MEMORY VERSES: PSALM 17:15; PSALM 63:1

First Kings catalogs a long list of kings of Israel and Judah. The evils of the kings of the divided kingdom climaxed with the rule of Ahab. First Kings 16:31 tells us that the sins of previous kings were trivial compared to Ahab's, which included worshiping Baal, building temples and altars to Baal, and marrying a priestess of Baal. As great as Ahab's sins were, the worst part was that he committed them while leading a nation, which means he led Israel down the same path. No wonder God was angry. It was into this darkness the Lord sent His prophet Elijah to proclaim the truth and judgment of God upon His people in a call for their repentance. Even amid some of Israel's darkest days, the Lord sent a light to His people and offered them a way out. He has done the same for us today through the light of the gospel.

As you read the Bible this week...

H IGHLIGHT the verses that speak to you.

Write out the name of the book:

Which chapter and verse numbers stand out to you?

E XPLAIN what this passage means.

To whom was it originally written? Why?

How does it fit with the verses before and after it?

What is the Holy Spirit intending to communicate through this text?

A PPLY what God is saying in these verses to your life.

What does this mean today?

What is God saying to you personally?

How can you apply this message to your life?

R ESPOND to what you've read.

In what ways does this passage call you to action?

How will you be different because of what you've learned?

Write out a prayer to God in response to what you read today:

102//1 KINGS 18–19

MEMORY VERSES: PSALM 17:15; PSALM 63:1

First Kings 18–19 describe some of the highs and lows of Elijah's ministry. God gave Elijah the responsibility to confront the idolatry in the land, so Elijah assembled Ahab and the prophets of Baal on Mount Carmel for a contest between God and Baal. Identical sacrifices were prepared and the deity who would send fire to consume His sacrifice would show Israel whom to worship. The prophets of Baal tried all day to coax their god to send fire, but nothing happened. After Elijah offered a simple prayer, God responded with fire, causing the people to recognize the power of the one true God. The events on the mountain enraged Jezebel, and she threatened to kill Elijah. He was forced to flee into the wilderness where he thought he would die. From his place of fear and hiding, though, Elijah listened to the quiet voice of the Lord, who reminded him of his calling and encouraged him to continue in his ministry. We all face challenges similar to the one Elijah presented on Mount Carmel and faced for himself in the wilderness. Will we choose God to be Lord of our lives, or will we be content to rely on our own abilities and resources? When we accept Christ as Savior, we still face daily choices of whether to seek and follow the Lord's guidance and to rely on His strength or to seek and rely on our own.

H

E

A

R

103//1 KINGS 21–22

MEMORY VERSES: PSALM 17:15; PSALM 63:1

The Book of 1 Kings closes with a picture of the full extent of Ahab's evil and the incomparable grace and mercy of God. Ahab desired the vineyard of a man named Naboth, but Naboth refused to sell it to him. As a result, Jezebel devised a plan to accuse Naboth falsely and have him stoned to death. After Naboth's death, Elijah condemned Ahab. The prophet said that the king's family would come to a disastrous end and that he and Jezebel would die violent deaths. That news led Ahab to do something he had never done before—repent of his sins and humble himself before God. With that demonstration of repentance, God postponed the family's destruction until after Ahab's death—an action that shows no one is outside the reach of God's grace and mercy. A few years later, Ahab asked King Jehoshaphat of Judah to join him in a war, but Jehoshaphat insisted on first hearing from God's prophets. While Jephoshaphat was well-intentioned, neither he nor Ahab listened to God's prophet Micaiah, who warned of defeat, and Ahab died in battle. From this story, it is Micaiah alone who stands out as an example of godly character, despite the love and grace God had shown Ahab. Micaiah's example reminds us that only by being transformed by faith in Christ are we able to understand God's will and receive the strength to stand firm on God's Word in the face of the world's pressures.

H

E

A

R

104//2 KINGS 2

MEMORY VERSES: PSALM 17:15; PSALM 63:1

The Book of 2 Kings picks up the story of the Northern and Southern Kingdoms where it left off at the end of 1 Kings. The first five chapters, however, focus on the ministry of the prophets, especially the transition from Elijah to his successor, Elisha. In chapter 2, we read of Elijah's exit from earth by being taken up to heaven in a chariot of fire. Elisha asked for and received a "double portion" of Elijah's spirit. After Elijah was gone, the biblical writer focused on Elisha as the Lord's prophet. Various events of miraculous healing and signs from the Lord are described in 2 Kings 2–4 as being performed by Elisha among the people. It is interesting to note how so many of Elisha's miraculous works closely parallel those of Jesus in the Gospels—healing, raising from the dead, feeding thousands, and so on. Elisha's miracles helped the people understand that he was God's prophet and that God had not abandoned them after He took Elijah away. The Gospels provide us with that same assurance today, as we are reminded of the great lengths God went to in order to demonstrate His love for us and to call us to faith in Him. Even after Jesus ascended to heaven, God sent His Holy Spirit who remains our source of hope and assurance even today.

H

E

A

R

105//2 KINGS 5; 6:1-23

MEMORY VERSES: PSALM 17:15; PSALM 63:1

Second Kings 5 tells the story of Naaman, an Aramean army commander who came to Israel seeking a cure for his skin disease. The Israelite king sent Naaman to Elisha, who in turn sent instructions for Naaman to wash in the Jordan River. Naaman balked at the idea because he, like many of us today, had too much pride to humble himself before this prophet. It took the persuasion of Naaman's servants to convince him to listen to and trust God's prophet and to follow his instructions. Naaman reminds us that we all are in need of God's healing power because of the way sin wreaks havoc in our lives. As Naaman's example shows, God is ready and willing to cleanse and restore us when we humbly approach Him with our need. After Naaman was healed, he tried to give Elisha a gift, but Elisha refused. The prophet's attendant Gehazi privately tried to get something from the commander. Consequently, Gehazi was stricken with a skin disease. The parallel reversal of fortunes that take place in Naaman's and Gehazi's lives remind us that God's power alone transforms us from being selfish and disobedient people to being humble and obedient children of God.

H

E

A

R

106//JONAH 1–2

MEMORY VERSES: PSALM 16:11; JOHN 11:25-26

This week we shift to a section of the Old Testament that includes short books by God's prophets. Jonah was one of these. God called the prophet Jonah to proclaim His message of judgment on Nineveh. However, Jonah chose instead to board a ship going in the opposite direction. Because he fled, the Lord sent a storm that brought Jonah face-to-face with his sin and a large fish. From inside the fish, Jonah agreed to be His prophet. One of the themes of the book is God's salvation. First the sailors were physically saved when God stopped the storm, then in chapter 2, Jonah was physically saved by God. This set the stage for spiritual salvation through repentance that was at the heart of Jonah's message to the Ninevites. God offers all people spiritual salvation through the work of Jesus who died on the cross to save us from our sins. Once we accept God's offer of salvation, we are to share the gospel with others.

As you read the Bible this week...

H I G H L I G H T the verses that speak to you.

Write out the name of the book:

Which chapter and verse numbers stand out to you?

E X P L A I N what this passage means.

To whom was it originally written? Why?

How does it fit with the verses before and after it?

What is the Holy Spirit intending to communicate through this text?

A P P L Y what God is saying in these verses to your life.

What does this mean today?

What is God saying to you personally?

How can you apply this message to your life?

R E S P O N D to what you've read.

In what ways does this passage call you to action?

How will you be different because of what you've learned?

Write out a prayer to God in response to what you read today:

107//JONAH 3–4

MEMORY VERSES: PSALM 16:11; JOHN 11:25-26

After the fish spit Jonah out alive, God repeated His command for the prophet to go to Nineveh and deliver a message to its people. This time Jonah did not hesitate. He warned the Ninevites of God's judgment against their sins, and the people responded by believing in God and repenting. Even the king repented and ordered the people to fast, pray, and change their sinful ways. However, Jonah's heart for the Ninevites had not changed, and he was furious that God saved this nation. While Jonah waited to see what God would do with the people, God used a shade plant to teach His prophet an important lesson about divine compassion. Jonah's story reminds us how important it is that we have hearts aligned with God's. God has made us His ambassadors to a dying world, which means we have to open our eyes to the countless people around us who desperately need the grace of God. As we mimic God's compassion, He will increase our heart for the lost and draw us closer to Himself.

H

E

A

R

108//HOSEA 1–3

MEMORY VERSES: PSALM 16:11; JOHN 11:25-26

Hosea was another of God's Old Testament prophets who was given a challenging task in order to communicate God's judgment and mercy to the people of Israel. To paint an incredibly symbolic picture, God commanded Hosea to marry a prostitute named Gomer as a representation of Israel's unfaithfulness to God. Hosea did as God told him, and the couple had three children who were each given a name that expressed a divine judgment against Israel. Besides judgment for sin, God also promised restoration—an important reminder of His faithfulness to His people despite their unfaithfulness to Him. Through Hosea, God promised that He would not give up on His people. Just as Hosea continually pursued Gomer through her unfaithfulness, God does the same for His people even today. God does more than pursue us, though; He redeems us with His love. As a symbol of God's redemptive love for Israel, He ordered Hosea to redeem and restore Gomer. Hosea's redemption of Gomer foreshadowed Jesus' redemption of us. On the cross, Jesus our Bridegroom made a way for us to experience forgiveness and redemption of our sins.

H

E

A

R

109//AMOS 1:1; 9

MEMORY VERSES: PSALM 16:11; JOHN 11:25-26

Each of God's Old Testament prophets had a specific purpose and focus for their ministry, and for Amos, that calling centered on the rampant idolatry and injustice in the Israelite community. From Amos 1:1, we learn that Amos was not a prophet by trade—he was a sheep breeder. Regardless, God used Amos to point out how far God's people had strayed from Him. Chapter 9 includes God's message of judgment against the people for their sins, but it also includes His message of hope. God, in His justice, had to punish the people for their sins, but He also promised that after the time of judgment, He would restore and repair the broken nation out of faithfulness to His covenant promises. God promised that "David's fallen booth" (9:11) would be restored—a promise that was ultimately fulfilled in Jesus, who descended from David's earthly line and brought about the justice and redemption the people needed desperately. Today we too place our hope in Christ for restoration and redemption. Through Christ, God calls us to repentance, just as He did the Israelites. He also calls us to stand up for the injustices in our world as Amos did.

H

E

A

R

110//JOEL 1–3

Although each of God's prophets had a unique calling, one common theme runs throughout all of these Old Testament books: God judges sin and calls His people to repentance. This surfaces again in the Book of Joel. A severe locust plague overtook Judah, an event Joel understood to be a sign of God's judgment against the people for their lack of concern and conviction over sin. One of the problems the people faced was their assumption that because they were descendants of Abraham, they would be safe from God's judgment, regardless of their behavior. But God, who is both righteous and just, could not ignore their sin, so out of compassion for His people He sent the plague as well as the prophecy of a coming invasion to draw them back to Himself. Again we see God's mercy on display when He promised to restore anyone who repented. God also promised His Holy Spirit who would serve as a sign of His mercy and relationship with them. The apostle Peter quoted Joel 2:28-32 during his Pentecost sermon to assure the people that God was faithful to fulfill the promise He had made (Acts 2:16-21). The Book of Joel reminds us of God's power and justice, two of His perfect attributes that are constantly at work in our lives. When we reflect on these traits, we are reminded of the grace God has shown us, and we should be brought to awe that He has chosen us to be His beloved children.

H

E

A

R

111//ISAIAH 6; 9

MEMORY VERSES: ISAIAH 53:5-6; 1 PETER 2:23-24

The heart of the Book of Isaiah is to demonstrate God's holiness and grace and issue a call for His people to return to Him in obedience and faith. Isaiah 6 records Isaiah's encounter with God when he was called to be a prophet. Isaiah's response to God's commission—"Here I am! Send me."—is one of the greatest pictures of obedience in all of Scripture. In Isaiah 9, we read the first of many Messianic prophecies in the book when God promised the birth of a child who would deliver His people. Matthew revealed in his Gospel that Isaiah's prophecy pointed to the birth of Jesus, the One who takes away the sins of the world. Despite our disobedience and sinfulness, God has given us a Redeemer in Jesus, and through Him, we gain eternal life in the presence of that same glorious God Isaiah witnessed.

As you read the Bible this week...

H I G H L I G H T the verses that speak to you.

Write out the name of the book:

Which chapter and verse numbers stand out to you?

E X P L A I N what this passage means.

To whom was it originally written? Why?

How does it fit with the verses before and after it?

What is the Holy Spirit intending to communicate through this text?

A P P L Y what God is saying in these verses to your life.

What does this mean today?

What is God saying to you personally?

How can you apply this message to your life?

R E S P O N D to what you've read.

In what ways does this passage call you to action?

How will you be different because of what you've learned?

Write out a prayer to God in response to what you read today:

112//ISAIAH 44—45

MEMORY VERSES: ISAIAH 53:5-6; 1 PETER 2:23-24

While the first half of Isaiah is about God's judgment for people's sins, the second half brings words of peace and hope to the people as He reminds them of His covenant by continuing to point them to the coming Messiah. In today's reading, God reminded the people that He chose them, and that He alone—not any of their man-made idols—has the power to restore them. With powerful imagery, God listed many ways that the people's idols were foolish and helpless to save them. Isaiah also prophesied about how King Cyrus of Persia would defeat the Babylonians and help bring God's people back from exile. These chapters remind us that God alone is the Creator and Sustainer of the world and that He orchestrates everything according to His will and good purposes. When life seems hopeless and God seems far away, God's faithfulness to His people throughout Scripture reminds us that He is always at work in our lives.

H

E

A

R

113//ISAIAH 52–53

MEMORY VERSES: ISAIAH 53:5-6; 1 PETER 2:23-24

Isaiah 52–53 is part of Isaiah's "Servant Song," a lengthy prophecy about Jesus, the Messiah and Suffering Servant of God. In these chapters, we read about God's solution for His people's sin problem: God would send His servant to suffer on humanity's behalf, an act that would bear the punishment for all human sin and extend forgiveness to all who would believe. Unlike the Israelites, who continued to fall into patterns of disobedience and lack of faith, the coming Servant would be obedient and faithful always, even at the cost of His own life. As people living on this side of the cross, we know that only Jesus, the Son of God, could live the perfect and sinless life necessary to be the sacrifice for our sins. When we reflect on the suffering Jesus endured and the lengths God went to in order to offer us forgiveness and eternal life in Him, we can't help but want to live our lives in service to Him.

H

E

A

R

114//ISAIAH 65–66

MEMORY VERSES: ISAIAH 53:5-6; 1 PETER 2:23-24

Through God's use of Isaiah, the Israelites were convicted of their sins, recognized God's faithful love, and prayed for Him to again look with favor upon them (Isa. 63–64). The book closes with God's response to Israel's prayer, which was a final reminder of His faithful love and their repeated disobedience. God used Isaiah to tell the people that they would be punished for their sins but that they would also be restored to Him, and eventually, that restoration would be eternal. As a result, people everywhere would recognize God for who He is and serve and worship Him in response. From the vision of the future in Revelation, we are reminded that one day this eternal worship will be a reality for all of God's people. And so, in the meantime, we are to serve God and live for Him today.

H

E

A

R

115//MICAH 1; 4:6-13; 5

MEMORY VERSES: ISAIAH 53:5-6; 1 PETER 2:23-24

The prophet Micah's ministry overlapped with Isaiah's and shared many of the same themes, but Micah targeted his prophecies at the southern kingdom, Judah. Like Isaiah, Micah's prophecies describe God's judgment of wickedness and His mercy for those who come to Him in repentance and faith. The main sin God spoke out against was idolatry. These were God's people, but they rejected Him and His laws by allowing and even participating in idol worship. As we saw in Isaiah, though, Micah also prophesied about the hope that would come through a Deliverer. Micah proclaims a few different Messianic prophecies about Jesus, including His birth in Bethlehem, His second coming, and His eternal reign. Some of these promises have already come to pass. However, we can have confidence in God today, knowing that He will be faithful to do what He has promised. The promised return of Jesus gives us the hope and strength we need to face all of life's present difficulties, and it should motivate us to live in daily obedience to Him.

H

E

A

R

116//2 KINGS 17–18

MEMORY VERSES: PROVERBS 29:18; JEREMIAH 1:15

God made a covenant with Abraham that He reiterated to Isaac and Jacob. It included plans for a portion of land where God's people would live. However, because of the people's repeated disobedience, they lost inheritance of the promised land. Through countless judges, prophets, and other leaders, God warned the people to turn back to Him, but they abandoned His invitation, causing God to allow them to be taken captive by the Assyrians. At the same time, King Hezekiah attempted to reform the southern kingdom of Judah by leading the people back to God. These chapters remind us that God's judgment is serious, but it is never without just cause: God had shown His people incredible grace, but they refused to turn to Him. Furthermore, Hezekiah is a reminder for us that no matter how tempted or pressured we may feel to turn our backs on God, we can always trust in His goodness and sovereignty over our lives.

As you read the Bible this week...

HIGHLIGHT the verses that speak to you.

Write out the name of the book:

Which chapter and verse numbers stand out to you?

EXPLAIN what this passage means.

To whom was it originally written? Why?

How does it fit with the verses before and after it?

What is the Holy Spirit intending to communicate through this text?

APPLY what God is saying in these verses to your life.

What does this mean today?

What is God saying to you personally?

How can you apply this message to your life?

RESPOND to what you've read.

In what ways does this passage call you to action?

How will you be different because of what you've learned?

Write out a prayer to God in response to what you read today:

117//2 KINGS 19–21

MEMORY VERSES: PROVERBS 29:18; JEREMIAH 1:15

Hezekiah was a man of God, as evidenced through his prayers. Hezekiah prayed to God for deliverance from Assyria, and God delivered the city. Later, when Hezekiah was suffering from a terminal illness, he prayed for God to remember his faithfulness, and God added 15 more years to his life. However, Hezekiah wasn't perfect, and when he acted prideful over his treasures (which were blessings from God that Hezekiah took for granted), the prophet Isaiah warned him that eventually Judah would experience a fate like Israel's, and all his treasures would be gone. After Hezekiah died, the nation was ruled by two of its most wicked kings to date. God warned that His judgment was pending. While God's grace and patience for His people is limitless, we all come to a place where we must face the consequences of our sins. In those moments, it is crucial to remember that God never holds his love and grace for us. We are the ones who have drifted from Him.

H

E

A

R

118//2 KINGS 22–23

MEMORY VERSES: PROVERBS 29:18; JEREMIAH 1:15

King Josiah stood in sharp contrast to his father Amon and his grandfather Manasseh, and as a result, significant cultural changes began to take place during Josiah's reign. While God's temple was being repaired, the Book of the Law—Genesis to Deuteronomy—was discovered, and upon hearing it read, Josiah realized the nation was guilty of breaking the covenant and in danger of divine wrath. God's Word has always had the power to bring sin to light and turn hardened hearts toward repentance. Josiah renewed the covenant before the people and initiated a spiritual reform movement that rid the nation of idolatry and renewed times of worship and celebration before God. While these were all positive changes, Josiah was the last righteous king of Judah. His death paved the way for the judgment against sin that God's prophets had warned against. Josiah's example reminds us that our obedience to God is rooted in our relationship with Him and our acceptance of the authority of His Word in our lives.

H

E

A

R

119//JEREMIAH 1–3:5

MEMORY VERSES: PROVERBS 29:18; JEREMIAH 1:15

Jeremiah became God's prophet during the reign of King Josiah and remained a prophet through the last of Judah's kings. This was a tumultuous time in the nation's history, and God had stern warnings He wanted His people to hear through His prophet. It is no surprise that Jeremiah was hesitant to obey God's calling. Jeremiah tried to avoid God's call with various excuses, but God revealed to the prophet that He had chosen him before birth for this very task. Idolatry—a violation of the first and second Commandments—was again revealed as the major sin the people were guilty of, which in turn created a rift in their relationship with God. Through Jeremiah, God offered the people yet another chance for repentance, but He also warned of the judgment that was coming. Like Jeremiah, our task as God's representatives today is to listen to His Word, obey His call, and share the truth of His love and the need for repentance with others.

H

E

A

R

120//JEREMIAH 25; 29

MEMORY VERSES: PROVERBS 29:18; JEREMIAH 1:15

For 23 years Jeremiah delivered the same call of repentance to the people of Judah time and time again, but the people refused to listen. Unfortunately, the time for God's judgment had come, and Jeremiah told them that the nation was about to be overpowered by the Babylonians. Jeremiah described a cup of God's wrath that all the wicked nations would drink as punishment from God, imagery that brings to mind Jesus' prayer in the garden of Gethsemane prior to His crucifixion: "My Father! If it is possible, let this cup pass from Me. Yet not as I will, but as You will" (Matt. 26:39). By going to the cross, Jesus drank the cup of God's wrath, taking all sin of humankind on Himself in order to satisfy God's divine justice. In Jeremiah 29, we also read that God used the prophet to provide hope to some of the people of Judah who had been taken into exile in Babylon. Jeremiah sent a letter to them, encouraging them to make the best of their situation because the exile would last for seventy years. Jeremiah warned the exiles not to listen to false promises and to find their hope instead in the Lord.

H

E

A

R

121//JEREMIAH 31:31-40; 32–33

MEMORY VERSES: EZEKIEL 36:26-27; DANIEL 4:35

The first part of Jeremiah contains prophecies about God's judgment against the people of Judah for their sins, but as the prophecies continue, the predictions shift to promises of God's restoration. Because God's love for the people was unending, He planned to establish a new covenant—one based on the transformation of their hearts rather than on laws engraved on stone tablets. The Lord would be with His people, and they would truly know Him. Chapters 32–33 record promises the Lord made concerning His restored people. He would give them a blessed and hopeful future. Nothing would be too difficult for the Lord to accomplish on their behalf. He would establish an unbreakable covenant with them. This new covenant is a reality for all Christians today, and it is based on the sacrifice of Jesus who made a way for us to have a personal relationship with God and the presence of the Holy Spirit in our lives.

As you read the Bible this week...

HIGHLIGHT the verses that speak to you.

Write out the name of the book:

Which chapter and verse numbers stand out to you?

EXPLAIN what this passage means.

To whom was it originally written? Why?

How does it fit with the verses before and after it?

What is the Holy Spirit intending to communicate through this text?

APPLY what God is saying in these verses to your life.

What does this mean today?

What is God saying to you personally?

How can you apply this message to your life?

RESPOND to what you've read.

In what ways does this passage call you to action?

How will you be different because of what you've learned?

Write out a prayer to God in response to what you read today:

122//JEREMIAH 52; 2 KINGS 24–25

MEMORY VERSES: EZEKIEL 36:26-27; DANIEL 4:35

Jeremiah's prophecies had predicted the fall of Jerusalem as God brought forth His judgment on the people. The Book of Jeremiah ends with a narrative of those events, which are also told in 2 Kings 24–25. Three months after Jehoiachin became king, the king of Babylon (Nebuchadnezzar) invaded Judah, took captive the king and his family as well as thousands of leading citizens, and installed Zedekiah, Jehoiachin's relative, as a puppet ruler. Thirty-seven years after being taken captive to Babylon, King Jehoiachin received a pardon from Evil-merodach, the new Babylonian ruler. Jehoiachin's life changed for the better, although he remained a king-in-exile for the rest of his life. Jehoiachin's release signaled the hope of restoration for Judah. God finally held the people of Judah accountable for their centuries of sin and rebellion against Him, but unlike His unfaithful people, God proved even in judgment that He was still faithful, and that in Him, we find restoration and hope.

H

E

A

R

123//EZEKIEL 1:1-3; 36:16-38; 37

MEMORY VERSES: EZEKIEL 36:26-27; DANIEL 4:35

With the fall of Jerusalem, the people of Judah were exiled to Babylon. The prophet Ezekiel delivered God's messages to His people while they were in exile, and he was an exile himself. At the heart of Ezekiel's prophecy is God's deliverance and restoration of His people (Ezek. 36:24-26). That God preserved a remnant of exiles from the Northern and Southern Kingdoms reminds us that He never allowed His people to be completely destroyed. Even though the ultimate consequence of sin is death, God kept a remnant for His glory and the good of the world. This restoration was the message behind Ezekiel's vision of the valley of dry bones in chapter 37. Instead of decomposition, God composes. Instead of decay, God restores. Through the power and truth of the Word of God and the presence of the Holy Spirit, you and I are becoming more alive each day. When we become Christians, God raises us from spiritual death. As our old nature is dying, our new nature is growing, and God is putting His words in our mouths so we can offer a message of hope and life within a world of death and decay.

H

E

A

R

124//DANIEL 1–2

MEMORY VERSES: EZEKIEL 36:26-27; DANIEL 4:35

Daniel was another of God's prophets who ministered during the exile in Babylon. The Babylonians took many young exiles captive and trained them to serve in the king's court. Daniel was one of these young men, but the actions he took in Daniel 1–2 show he had no plan to adopt the Babylonian faith. Daniel and his three friends disciplined themselves to eat only vegetables and drink water so as not to compromise their faithfulness to God in the matter of dietary laws. God gave the faithful young men knowledge, understanding, and wisdom, enabling them to serve wisely for many years. The dream Daniel interpreted in Daniel 2 focused on kingdoms: the power of Nebuchadnezzar's kingdom and a future greater kingdom that would never end. Daniel's interpretation was looking to Jesus Christ, who would institute a new kingdom and whose reign would never end. From the beginning of this prophetic book, we see that God's people can trust in God's power and control along with the goodness of His Word.

H

E

A

R

125//DANIEL 3–4

MEMORY VERSES: EZEKIEL 36:26-27; DANIEL 4:35

Daniel 3 records the popular event of three Jewish men—Shadrach, Meshach, and Abednego—who refused to compromise their faith in God. Nebuchadnezzar made a huge statue and demanded everyone bow down to it. To refuse to worship the statue meant disobeying the king's decree, the same as disobeying the king himself. Shadrach, Meshach, and Abednego meant no disrespect to the king. Their failure to bow down to the gold statue was motivated by their relationship with the one true God. The determination of Shadrach, Meshach, and Abednego was matched only by Nebuchadnezzar's rage at their refusal to obey him. In anger, he ordered the men to be thrown into a furnace of fire. But when they were, nothing went as planned. Nebuchadnezzar witnessed first-hand God's presence with His servants in the fiery furnace, and the men emerged unscathed. In chapter 4, the very authority that he attempted to overrule humbled Nebuchadnezzar. As a result, a pagan king was forced to bow down to the holy God. We are reminded that God is present with His people in every threatening situation and uses their faithfulness to glorify His name. Also, we are warned against claiming authority that doesn't belong to us.

H

E

A

R

126//DANIEL 5–6

MEMORY VERSES: DANIEL 6:26-27; DANIEL 9:19

Daniel 5 begins with a feast thrown by King Belshazzar. When Belshazzar saw a cryptic message written on the wall, God used Daniel to interpret the vision and point out Belshazzar's failure to honor the one true God. Because of the powers Daniel displayed, he was singled out by officials who felt threatened by him, and these men watched for an opportunity to pit Daniel against the king. Knowing Daniel's faith in God, they manipulated the king to force everyone to pray only to him, with the punishment of disobedience being death in a lion's den. Daniel maintained his discipline of prayer even though doing so brought a death sentence. When the king found Daniel alive the next morning, he worshiped God and cast the "wise men" to the lions. As we practice the discipline of prayer, we will grow in our faith, trusting that God can help us face any situation with courage. Prayer will prove to be a lifeline of communication with God.

As you read the Bible this week...

HIGHLIGHT the verses that speak to you.

Write out the name of the book:

Which chapter and verse numbers stand out to you?

EXPLAIN what this passage means.

To whom was it originally written? Why?

How does it fit with the verses before and after it?

What is the Holy Spirit intending to communicate through this text?

APPLY what God is saying in these verses to your life.

What does this mean today?

What is God saying to you personally?

How can you apply this message to your life?

RESPOND to what you've read.

In what ways does this passage call you to action?

How will you be different because of what you've learned?

Write out a prayer to God in response to what you read today:

127//DANIEL 9–10; 12

In addition to demonstrating a life of faithfulness to God through strenuous circumstances, the Book of Daniel includes several chapters of prophecy concerning end times events. As these prophetic visions of judgment and tribulation unfolded, Daniel prayed for God's forgiveness, repeatedly confessing the sins of the people (Dan. 9). Among the specific things God revealed to Daniel was a time of international turmoil that resulted in the persecution and death of some of His people. There is hope, though, and the time of conflict in persecution will come to an end. Eternal life awaits those whose names are found written in the book, but eternal shame for those who rebelled against God. This eternal life—secured for us through the sacrificial life, death, and resurrection of Jesus—is the source of ultimate hope and confidence for every believer of Christ. We know that Jesus will come again and make eternal life in the presence of God our eternal reality, and until then, we are to live out our mission of being His disciples in a lost and hopeless world.

H

E

A

R

128//EZRA 1-2

Just as God brought destruction upon the city of Jerusalem through the destruction of the temple of the Lord, so He brought about the eventual restoration of the temple and the return of the exiles as recorded in Ezra. For the first period of the Israelites' return, the Lord spoke to Cyrus, the king of Persia, who also happened to be a Gentile non-believer. It was through Cyrus that the Lord made the return of His people possible. Cyrus offered reentry into the land to anyone who would help rebuild the temple, to which he was also going to restore all of the treasures stolen from the original temple by Nebuchadnezzar. The Lord's divine plan is evident through both the exile and return of the people to Jerusalem. This is especially evident in His use of Cyrus to be an instrument for His divine will. Even a Persian king recognized the power, control, and sovereignty of the God of the universe. Like the Jews who responded to the opportunity, we should respond with joy, gratitude, and determination to the opportunities God gives us to be a part of His work also.

H

E

A

R

129//EZRA 3–4

Just months after leaving Babylon, the exiles had rebuilt the altar and restored the formal forms of worship given through Moses. They also hired laborers and purchased building materials so the temple could be rebuilt. The Lord's help was evident in laying the temple's foundation, and they used that as an opportunity for worship and to bring glory to His name. The Jews praised God by declaring His essential character. Their joy came because they seized the opportunity God gave to participate in His work. But credit for the work's success was due to God, not the people. Soon after the exiles arrived in Jerusalem, word of their endeavor reached people living near the ruined city, and opposition to the rebuilding efforts quickly arose. People approached Zerubbabel with an offer of help, but in reality, they opposed the Jewish effort and intended to sabotage it. This opposition brought construction to a standstill, and nothing proceeded for well over a decade. Despite our faithfulness to God, we are guaranteed opposition to His work in the world. As this part of God's story reminds us, opposition cannot hinder God's faithfulness to His people or His purposes.

H

E

A

R

130//EZRA 5–6

Finally, after more than a decade, construction resumed on the temple. The building activity in Jerusalem raised suspicion among local Persian officials. They allowed the work to continue while they investigated. Discovery of Cyrus' decree insured the completion of the temple. When restoration of the temple was complete, the people participated in Passover, which marked the renewal of religious life for the Jews, who could once again worship in obedience to God's Word. The restored exiles had many reasons for being joyful. Primarily, the Lord made them joyful because the Persian king's attitude had changed. We too should rejoice in a God who directs the rule of human kings. Since the time of the garden of Eden when sin entered the world, God has been restoring His people to Himself, and He continues to do so today. At the heart of our restoration is repentance of sin and obedience to Him.

H

E

A

R

131//ZECHARIAH 1:1-6; 2; 12

MEMORY VERSES: ZEPHANIAH 3:17; 1 PETER 3:15

Zechariah was one of God's prophets appointed to deliver His messages to the Jews who returned to Jerusalem after the exile. God sent Zechariah to encourage the people to continue work on the temple even in the face of opposition. Through a series of visions to Zechariah, God revealed His purposes. He would restore their city and their relationship with Him, and eventually He would give Israel final victory over its enemies. These verses also contain God's promise of a Messiah and His promise to pour out the Spirit of grace on the people of Jerusalem. These prophecies point to Jesus—the One who was pierced on the cross for the sins of mankind, and the One through whom final victory against sin and death is accomplished. Zechariah also prophesied the coming of the Holy Spirit. As believers, we can rejoice that salvation in Christ brings peace today and hope for eternal peace tomorrow.

As you read the Bible this week...

HIGHLIGHT the verses that speak to you.

Write out the name of the book:

Which chapter and verse numbers stand out to you?

EXPLAIN what this passage means.

To whom was it originally written? Why?

How does it fit with the verses before and after it?

What is the Holy Spirit intending to communicate through this text?

APPLY what God is saying in these verses to your life.

What does this mean today?

What is God saying to you personally?

How can you apply this message to your life?

RESPOND to what you've read.

In what ways does this passage call you to action?

How will you be different because of what you've learned?

Write out a prayer to God in response to what you read today:

132//EZRA 7–8

ZEPHANIAH 3:17; 1 PETER 3:15

Ezra 7–8 tells about the return to Jerusalem for the second group of exiles from Babylon, this time led by Ezra himself. Ezra was a scribe who lived as an exile in the area of Babylon, and he longed to see his homeland again. A new Persian king, Artaxerxes I, finally gave Ezra permission to lead a delegation of exiles back home. Their task was to reestablish proper worship of "the God of heaven." God's providential hand appears in every act leading to the return of His people and the restoration of the nation. God not only used faithful believers like Ezra, but also moved pagan rulers like Artaxerxes to participate in His plan. Ezra wanted to implement a spiritual revival in Israel. God's people were meant to lead the way in demonstrating what life can be like when lived in accordance with God and His Word. Today, we have the opportunity to obey God and to show a lost world how abundant life can be through faith in Jesus Christ and faithfulness to God's Word.

H

E

A

R

133//EZRA 9–10

After settling into Jerusalem, Ezra received an official report on affairs in Judah, but what Ezra heard was devastating. Instead of living as God's chosen and set-apart people, men had married foreign wives, which was in direct opposition to God's covenant. This issue was not one of race or nationalism; it was a spiritual problem because the women worshiped false gods. Casual acceptance of these religions by husbands denied the Lord's claim that He alone was God. Consequently, the nation the Lord commanded to be holy had become no different from its pagan neighbors. Ezra grieved over how far God's people had fallen, and his very public grief moved many people to confession of sins and repentance. Like Ezra, we need to be people who are grieved over the presence of sin in our lives and the lives of our loved ones. God has chosen us and set us apart for His glory and to be lights for Him in our world. Only with a healthy view of our sin can we live the life of repentance and obedience to God that He calls us to live for our own good and His glory.

H

E

A

R

134//ESTHER 1–2

The events described in the Book of Esther cover a 10-year period during the reign of Xerxes I, also known as Ahasuerus. Ahasuerus was an arrogant ruler, and when his queen refused to put herself on display at a lavish and drunken banquet, the king deposed her and launched an empire-wide search for a replacement. The quest for a new queen lasted four years. Esther was brought before Ahasuerus as part of this search. The king loved Esther—she won his favor and was selected as his new queen. Esther's unusual story is a clear picture of God's protection and care of His covenant people. Esther was a Jew God placed in a position to influence the destiny of His people and nations at a time when they would need an advocate. Even in our most trying situations, God is always at work for our long term good, even if in the short term it is not clear how He's doing so. He wants His people to trust Him wholeheartedly and confidently—even in the midst of radical, unexpected change.

H

E

A

R

135//ESTHER 3—4

MEMORY VERSES: ZEPHANIAH 3:17; 1 PETER 3:15

The plot of the Book of Esther thickens with the introduction of the villain, a man named Haman who held a powerful position in the king's court. Haman descended from a Canaanite tribe that consistently opposed Israel, from the exodus out of Egypt to the reign of David. When Mordecai failed to show Haman the respect he desired, he determined to eliminate all the Jews from the empire. Haman persuaded King Ahasuerus that the Jews threatened the Persian Empire's national security. He obtained a royal decree, setting aside a time for slaughtering the Jewish people. But God had placed Esther in a situation in which she could make an astounding difference so long as she trusted Him. Mordecai challenged Esther with the truth that God had a specific purpose in placing her in her royal position. God will not fail to keep His promises or fall short of His purposes. Therefore, the deliverance of the Jews was certain. The only question was what Esther's role would be. God had made her queen so that she could deliver His people through His provision. Esther's account serves as a reminder that God places people where they can serve Him.

H

E

A

R

136//ESTHER 5–7

MEMORY VERSES: DEUTERONOMY 29:29; PSALM 101:3-4

Esther decided to intervene for her people. The stakes were high. Even the queen could be put to death for entering the king's presence without an invitation. So Esther prepared through fasting and praying. The Jewish people did the same. After three days, Esther entered the king's court, inviting the king and Haman to a banquet. Her patience gave time for God to work out the details of His plan for salvation. Time and again in Scripture, we are reminded that God orchestrates even the seemingly insignificant moments of our lives to bring Him glory. Whereas Haman was expecting to be honored by his enemy Mordecai, it was Mordecai who would be publicly honored by Haman. Throughout, we are reminded of God's sovereign control over the details of our lives. As you reflect on the picture of God in these chapters, remember that God is in control of your life, which means you can trust Him wholeheartedly.

As you read the Bible this week...

H IGHLIGHT the verses that speak to you.

Write out the name of the book:

Which chapter and verse numbers stand out to you?

E XPLAIN what this passage means.

To whom was it originally written? Why?

How does it fit with the verses before and after it?

What is the Holy Spirit intending to communicate through this text?

A PPLY what God is saying in these verses to your life.

What does this mean today?

What is God saying to you personally?

How can you apply this message to your life?

R ESPOND to what you've read.

In what ways does this passage call you to action?

How will you be different because of what you've learned?

Write out a prayer to God in response to what you read today:

137//ESTHER 8–10

MEMORY VERSES: DEUTERONOMY 29:29; PSALM 101:3-4

Esther exposed Haman's plot which led Ahasuerus to have him executed. But the edict to kill the Jews remained in effect. Under Persian law, Ahasuerus could not revoke it. Instead, the king issued a second edict authorizing Jews to arm and defend themselves, unleashing two days of violence as the two sides fought openly. The Jews overcame their opposition, and afterward, Mordecai ordered a celebration of these victories, which led to the establishment of the annual Festival of Purim. Because of the faithfulness of Esther and Mordecai, the Jewish people were protected, and God received the glory for everything He had done. Although the name of God is never explicitly mentioned in Esther, the book emphasizes the providence of God, the power of prayer and fasting, and the persuasive potential of courageous men and women of faith. God used Mordecai and Esther in a mighty way to preserve His covenant people—and with them, His ultimate plan of deliverance that would come nearly five centuries later in Jesus Christ. As their story reminds us, God receives glory when His people live in faithful obedience to Him.

H

E

A

R

138//NEHEMIAH 1–2

MEMORY VERSES: DEUTERONOMY 29:29; PSALM 101:3-4

The Book of Nehemiah picks up where Ezra left off in the historical records of the restoration of Jerusalem. Under Ezra's spiritual leadership, the Jews began to renew their allegiance to the Lord. Just 13 years later, Artaxerxes allowed another Jewish leader, Nehemiah, to return to the city. Nehemiah appeared with an ambitious goal: to rebuild the city's wall. Nearly a century had passed since the first Jewish exiles returned to Jerusalem. In that time they had constructed the temple and various other, mostly private, structures. Yet even so, the defensive wall that surrounded the city remained to be rebuilt. The true problem wasn't a broken-down city. The true problem was a broken-down people who had a disconnected relationship with God. Nehemiah was called to rebuild a city and a community of people in shambles. Because of the exile, Jerusalem was in need of both physical and spiritual renewal. The same is true of our broken world. There are hurting and helpless people all around us—people who need the hope of Christ. When we let this reality sink in, like Nehemiah, we are compelled to step up and make a difference.

H

E

A

R

139//NEHEMIAH 3–4

MEMORY VERSES: DEUTERONOMY 29:29; PSALM 101:3-4

The work to which God called Nehemiah would not be easy. And he could not do it alone. One reason the work progressed so quickly was that everyone took part, from rulers and temple personnel to merchants and families. Even people from the villages distant from Jerusalem helped. More intimidating than the physical obstacles was the human opposition. Not everyone was thrilled with Nehemiah's plan. In the Persian government, lines of authority were not always clear, and some officials feared that a stronger Jerusalem would diminish their prestige. For others, the development awakened ancient rivalries with the Jews. These enemies would seek to undermine Nehemiah with false accusations. Many people living in the vicinity were determined to spoil Nehemiah's plans. When we commit to faithfully serving God, He gives us big, God-sized goals that are only accomplished when we depend on Him. Oftentimes, the bigger the goal, the bigger the challenges we face. No matter the source of our opposition, God gives us the strength to persevere and complete our tasks, as Nehemiah and the people of Jerusalem demonstrated for us.

H

E

A

R

140//NEHEMIAH 5-6

MEMORY VERSES: DEUTERONOMY 29:29; PSALM 101:3-4

During the building program, Nehemiah learned of social injustice among the Jewish population. The number of workers needed to rebuild Jerusalem's wall was immense. The danger of attack required an equal number of men for military service. The economic strain created by pulling so many able-bodied workers from the regular labor force gave way to corruption. Some Jews took advantage of other Jews to increase their profits. Nehemiah knew that the wall would not be completed unless the needs of the people were met. But more importantly, he knew that the rebuilding of the "spiritual city" would never be completed unless he faced the issues at hand. Despite external opposition and internal problems, the people continued to build the wall. Finally, the work was finished. It had taken only 52 days. From the beginning, Nehemiah had put the matter of rebuilding Jerusalem's wall in God's hands. God's people had determined that the best answer to their opposition was to keep working and to fulfill God's will. As they did so, neighboring nations saw God's power at work in them. When God's people accomplish God's work in God's strength, God gets the glory.

H

E

A

R

141//NEHEMIAH 7–8

MEMORY VERSES: NEHEMIAH 6:9; NEHEMIAH 9:6

Nehemiah 7–8 describes the steps the people took after building the wall. The wall was necessary, but Jerusalem would not remain safe without people. In Nehemiah 8, we read that after the people were settled, they devoted a day to hear the Word of God read to them from Ezra—a practice that was important because the people did not have prior access to Scripture. Today, reading God's Word should be taken just as seriously. Through Scripture, God reveals who He is and what obedience to Him looks like. Scripture also provides countless stories of people who have gone before us in faith and how God has proven faithful to His people time and again. The most important thing we learn through Scripture, though, is the one big story it tells—the story of God's work to redeem His people and draw them back to Him, which He accomplishes through the death, resurrection, and final victory of Jesus.

As you read the Bible this week...

HIGHLIGHT the verses that speak to you.

Write out the name of the book:

Which chapter and verse numbers stand out to you?

EXPLAIN what this passage means.

To whom was it originally written? Why?

How does it fit with the verses before and after it?

What is the Holy Spirit intending to communicate through this text?

APPLY what God is saying in these verses to your life.

What does this mean today?

What is God saying to you personally?

How can you apply this message to your life?

RESPOND to what you've read.

In what ways does this passage call you to action?

How will you be different because of what you've learned?

Write out a prayer to God in response to what you read today:

142//NEHEMIAH 9

MEMORY VERSES: NEHEMIAH 6:9; NEHEMIAH 9:6

As the Israelites heard the Word of God read to them, they were reminded of God's faithfulness to His people and His plans, but they were also reminded of their unfaithfulness to Him. The sins of their ancestors were responsible for God's judgment against Jerusalem, which is what landed them in exile and necessitated the reconstruction of the city to begin with. Among the things Ezra's reading brought to light was the need for confession and repentance. Jesus once said, "Unless you repent, you will all perish as well" (Luke 13:3,5). Repentance can be defined as a heartfelt sorrow for sin, a renouncing of that sin, and a sincere commitment to turn from it and walk in obedience to Christ. Even as Christians, we often choose paths that lead us away from the Lord. We must accept responsibility for wandering away from God. No matter how badly we have stumbled in sin, the Lord lovingly invites us to return to Him. We cannot truly worship the Lord until we receive His forgiveness for the sin separating us from Him.

H

E

A

R

143//NEHEMIAH 10

MEMORY VERSES: NEHEMIAH 6:9; NEHEMIAH 9:6

Nehemiah 9 involved a time of worship and confession, and it ended by mentioning a covenant the people made with God in light of His provisions and their repentance. The people's covenant with God expressed their commitment to living in obedience to Him and His laws. After renewing their commitment to obey God and His laws, chapter 10 includes several specific promises the people made to show how they would live out this commitment in daily life. The promises, which cover everything from Sabbath practices to sacrifice rituals to tithing, reinforce the idea that God has set apart the Israelites to be His chosen people, and as such, they are to live holy and set-apart lives for Him. The goal is that they would be a witness to their community of the power and holiness of the one true God. Similarly, God calls us to live holy and set-apart lives, which we do when we live in obedience to Him, pursue Christ, and allow the Holy Spirit to transform us. As God's chosen people today, we are to continue to live as a light for Him in our dark and broken world.

H

E

A

R

144//NEHEMIAH 11

MEMORY VERSES: NEHEMIAH 6:9; NEHEMIAH 9:6

After the work of rebuilding the wall, God called certain people to relocate to Jerusalem and serve Him there. This was not necessarily the most desirable place to be. For most people, it meant relocating their families from the surrounding villages and uprooting their lives. Nehemiah instructed the people to cast lots to determine which families should go. Nehemiah 11 teaches that where you live and work matters to God. He has placed His people in specific places around specific people in order to serve Him uniquely. In his letter to the Colossian believers, Paul wrote, "Whatever you do, do it enthusiastically, as something done for the Lord and not for men" (Col. 3:23). This verse reminds us that, for the Christian, all of life is about glorying God and serving Him—there should be no difference in your secular duty and your sacred duty. Our attitude toward work makes a great deal of difference. As Christians, we can and should add an eternal perspective to our viewpoint. We know our ultimate reward for a job well done will come from the Lord.

H

E

A

R

145//NEHEMIAH 12

MEMORY VERSES: NEHEMIAH 6:9; NEHEMIAH 9:6

The completion of the wall and the repopulation of the city were celebrated with a dedication of the wall. This included singing, ritual purification, and a procession around the wall led by Nehemiah. The people recognized that their ability to rebuild the wall so quickly amid such opposition was possible only because of the Lord, so they worshiped Him with songs of thanksgiving and praise. The climax of the celebration was the presentation of offerings to Him. We live in a culture that values individualism and a "pull yourself up by the bootstraps" mentality, which hinders us from acknowledging that even our best efforts and accomplishments are the result of God's blessing and provision in our lives. Every gift, talent, and opportunity you have is a result of God's desire to be glorified through your life, which He knows will alone lead to your greatest fulfillment and joy. Think about your offerings—everything from your monetary tithe to the way you spend your talents and time. Are you living like God is the source of everything you have? If not, it's time for a change.

H

E

A

R

146//NEHEMIAH 13

MEMORY VERSES: PSALM 51:17; COLOSSIANS 1:19-20

The Book of Nehemiah concludes with an update from Nehemiah about what occurred in the newly revived city after he left. Nehemiah was governor in Jerusalem for 12 years. Upon completing his mission, Nehemiah returned to Babylon to serve King Artaxerxes as he had promised. After some time, Nehemiah's thoughts returned to Jerusalem. He was granted a second term as governor of the city, but when he returned he discovered violations of God's laws. The people strayed from the promises they made when they renewed their covenant. Once again, Nehemiah found himself helping the people of God restore their relationship with Him. At its heart, the book is about the restoration of a city and the restoration of the people of God. It challenges us to evaluate our spiritual lives, get rid of the things that are separating us from God, and take steps toward restoration through trust and obedience to Him.

As you read the Bible this week...

HIGHLIGHT the verses that speak to you.

Write out the name of the book:

Which chapter and verse numbers stand out to you?

EXPLAIN what this passage means.

To whom was it originally written? Why?

How does it fit with the verses before and after it?

What is the Holy Spirit intending to communicate through this text?

APPLY what God is saying in these verses to your life.

What does this mean today?

What is God saying to you personally?

How can you apply this message to your life?

RESPOND to what you've read.

In what ways does this passage call you to action?

How will you be different because of what you've learned?

Write out a prayer to God in response to what you read today:

147//MALACHI 1

MEMORY VERSES: PSALM 51:17; COLOSSIANS 1:19-20

Malachi was the last of the Old Testament prophets. He prophesied at the same time Ezra and Nehemiah were leading God's people. Four centuries of prophetic silence followed his proclamation. The next prophet to speak in Scripture for the Lord would be John the Baptist. Malachi predicted John's coming and also the coming of Jesus Christ, the Messiah. God's last recorded word through His prophets before the coming of Jesus into the world was for His people to honor Him with their hearts and to serve Him faithfully with their lives. The Book of Malachi begins with an emphasis on the greatness of God as seen in His love for His people. One of the first issues Malachi raised was God's accusation that Israel's priests disrespected Him by offering defiled sacrifices. Those offerings revealed a contemptible attitude toward God. Malachi's warning reminds us that God's greatness requires from us a worthy gift and a loving giver. We need to have a wholehearted love for God and show that love through our actions and through worship that is worthy of His name.

H

E

A

R

148//MALACHI 2

MEMORY VERSES: PSALM 51:17; COLOSSIANS 1:19-20

In Malachi 2, the prophet addressed specific sins of the priests and the people who were compromising their commitments to God—commitments that God takes very seriously. The priests were to revere God's name, give the people true instructions, live before God in peace and fairness, and turn the people from sin. They had done none of the above. Additionally, the people of Israel were the family of God; instead of honoring their family commitments to God and to one another, they were compromising those commitments by marrying people who worshiped idols and accepting their practices. God rebuked them and threatened to remove them from the community. God has called us all to serve Him in some way. Whatever position or avenue of service you've accepted in response to God's leading is a covenant made with Him. God calls us to live honorably for Him by setting godly examples in our relationships and obligations, and Malachi's words remind us He takes it very seriously when we do not.

H

E

A

R

149//MALACHI 3

MEMORY VERSES: PSALM 51:17; COLOSSIANS 1:19-20

At the close of Malachi 2, God charged His people with making Him weary by their words. The people charged God with injustice, an accusation that goes against His very character. He also accused them of robbing Him by not giving Him the tithes and offerings He is due. Sometimes we look at the state of the world around us and wonder if anything we do really makes a difference. We can understand where the people of Israel were coming from. They looked at the world around them and saw wicked people prospering, causing them to wonder what benefit there was to serving God. Like the Israelites, we often fail to recognize the goodness of God when things get difficult. It is into that discouraging place that God spoke a word of hope to His people—He would send His messenger (John the Baptist) and then He Himself would come to them and make things right, which He has done through Jesus. Today, as we hold out hope for Jesus' promised return, God still expects His people to remain faithful to Him, which we demonstrate by serving God with right attitudes and right actions.

H

E

A

R

150//MALACHI 4

MEMORY VERSES: PSALM 51:17; COLOSSIANS 1:19-20

At the close of Malachi's prophecy, God reminded the people that a final day of judgment and blessing was coming. God described this as a day when the wicked (those who did not follow God) would be consumed and the righteous (those who follow God) would be healed and their victory over evil complete. Before that day, Elijah would appear to prepare people for the coming day. About five centuries after Malachi lived, both an angel (Luke 1:16-17) and Jesus (Matt. 17:10-13) confirmed that John the Baptist fulfilled Malachi's prophecy of an Elijah who was to come. John was not Elijah in such a literal sense (John 1:21). Instead, John the Baptist loved the Lord wholeheartedly as Elijah did, turned people back to the Lord as Elijah did, and prepared the way for the Lord to come to His people as Elijah exemplified. Tucked into these final verses of the Old Testament is the hope of the gospel. The only thing that could finally preserve people from God's judgment against sin is for Jesus to bear the curse for us. He accomplished this in His death on the cross in fulfillment of Malachi's prophecy.

H

E

A

R

151//LUKE 1

MEMORY VERSES: JOHN 1:1-2; JOHN 1:14

For centuries God spoke through His prophets. Then after Malachi, He stopped. For nearly 500 years God remained silent. All of the promises God made seemed to be fading from the hearts of His people. He eventually spoke again through John the Baptist, a prophet who had the unique responsibility of announcing that Jesus, the long-awaited Messiah, had arrived. Luke began his Gospel with the angelic announcements of two key births—John the Baptist and Jesus. The birth stories of these two people were intricately linked. The angel's descriptions reveal key information about who Jesus is and why He came. Jesus is the Son of God. He came to save God's people from their sin and to establish the kingdom of God—His justice and righteousness—on earth. The announcement of Jesus' birth shows that God had not and would never abandon His people—a truth we need constant reminders of today.

As you read the Bible this week...

H I G H L I G H T the verses that speak to you.

Write out the name of the book:

Which chapter and verse numbers stand out to you?

E X P L A I N what this passage means.

To whom was it originally written? Why?

How does it fit with the verses before and after it?

What is the Holy Spirit intending to communicate through this text?

A P P L Y what God is saying in these verses to your life.

What does this mean today?

What is God saying to you personally?

How can you apply this message to your life?

R E S P O N D to what you've read.

In what ways does this passage call you to action?

How will you be different because of what you've learned?

Write out a prayer to God in response to what you read today:

152//LUKE 2

Luke 2 provides the account of Jesus' birth and childhood. Mary gave birth to Jesus in Bethlehem, an event that became a reason for celebration by the greatest and the least in heaven and on earth. An angel reported the good news to shepherds with a heavenly host singing God's praises. After Jesus' birth, Mary and Joseph fulfilled the important Jewish rites of the circumcision and purification sacrifice at the temple in Jerusalem. At age 12, Jesus traveled with Mary and Joseph to the temple. He spent time talking with the teachers, who were amazed at His wisdom. He then returned with His family to Nazareth. From the very beginning of Jesus' story, we learn that God's Son would not fit people's expectations of the Messiah, the great Deliverer and Conqueror of the Jews. In fact, we quickly realize that the invitation to know Jesus extends to everyone, regardless of class, education, race, or position. God has limitless, unconditional, and equal love for all of us. Likewise, we're called to have the same unconditional mindset as we're sent out to share the gospel.

H

E

A

R

153//MATTHEW 1–2

MEMORY VERSES: JOHN 1:1-2; JOHN 1:14

Each of the Gospels gives a detailed account of Jesus' time on earth; however, each writer had a unique purpose for writing that shaped which encounters and teachings they included. It also determined how they began and ended their Gospel. The Gospel of Matthew is written to a Jewish audience who had an understanding of Old Testament Scriptures. This explains why Matthew began with Jesus' genealogy, which affirms that Jesus descended from Abraham, Judah, and David, fulfilling various Old Testament prophecies about the Messiah. Following the genealogy, Matthew focused on events surrounding Jesus' birth. The angel's appearance to Joseph in a dream with the message of the miraculous conception underscores Jesus' divine nature. The wise men's search, discovery, and worship of Jesus further confirms His identity. Even the family's escape to Egypt, return to Israel, and their settling in Nazareth is a prophetic fulfillment. From reading about Jesus' birth and childhood in Matthew, we are reminded God keeps His promises. We also learn that Jesus was God's unique Son and that He alone is positioned to change the world.

H

E

A

R

154//MARK 1

MEMORY VERSES: JOHN 1:1-2; JOHN 1:14

Unlike the other three Gospels, Mark begins abruptly at the start of Jesus' earthly ministry, 30 years after His birth. Much of Mark's Gospel focuses on the actions of Jesus and how people responded to Him. The book begins with information about the preparations made for Jesus' ministry. John the Baptist called for repentance from sin and proclaimed the One (Jesus) to follow. Jesus presented Himself for baptism to John as a way of affirming John's ministry. Mark next introduced Jesus as proclaimer of the message of good news with a call to repentance. Jesus issues a formal invitation to four fisherman to follow Him. Jesus further demonstrated His oneness with God as He displayed authority over unclean spirits and healed many physical illnesses. Although many people sought Him because of His healing power, Jesus shied away from the crowds and devoted most of His time to training the twelve disciples. A final healing, however, shows Jesus' ministry to be marked by compassion toward those in need. From the beginning of Mark's gospel, we see that in Jesus' ministry, meeting people's spiritual and physical needs go hand in hand. This is the model He demonstrates for us.

H _____

E _____

_____

_____

A _____

_____

R _____

_____

155//JOHN 1

JOHN 1:1-2; JOHN 1:14

John 1 focuses on Jesus' divinity and role in creation as well as the start of His earthly ministry. The Word, Jesus, is divine, distinct from God the Father but one with Him. God created everything through the Word. Nothing came into being without His direct involvement. Life came through Jesus, who provided the light of God's love and guidance. As physical light dispelled the darkness on the first day of creation (Gen. 1:3), so Jesus' light pierced through the darkness of sin to provide eternal salvation to those who believe in Him. Although the world had been created through the Word, the world's people did not recognize or respond to Him. Despite that rejection, some accepted Jesus, believing in Him as Savior. In addition, John's Gospel also emphasizes the humanity of Jesus. By coming in human form, Jesus allowed us to see the glory of God. John the Baptist's witness proved true as the life, ministry, death, and resurrection of Jesus revealed God's grace and truth. In Him, we find grace, truth, and salvation. Like the first disciples who answered Jesus' call to follow Him, once Christ changes our lives, we are compelled to live for opportunities to demonstrate the power of the gospel, pointing others to Jesus.

H

E

A

R

156//MATTHEW 3–4

MEMORY VERSES: MATTHEW 5:16; MATTHEW 6:33

Before Jesus begins His public ministry, Matthew introduces John the Baptist, who prepared the way for Jesus by proclaiming a message of repentance and calling people to baptism as a symbol of their heart transformation. Jesus traveled to the river for John to baptize Him. Here, Jesus identified Himself with John's message and with the people He came to save. It is interesting to note that all three Persons of the Trinity show up for this important moment, which affirms that Jesus is the Son of God and that His mission is anointed by the Holy Spirit. After His baptism, Jesus endured a time of temptation in the desert. This preparation for ministry reveals the reality of the spiritual battle raging around us and provides a concrete example of how God equips us to withstand temptations. When we face temptations, we too can trust in the character of God and the promises of Scripture, no matter how appealing that temptation might be.

As you read the Bible this week...

H I G H L I G H T the verses that speak to you.

Write out the name of the book:

Which chapter and verse numbers stand out to you?

E X P L A I N what this passage means.

To whom was it originally written? Why?

How does it fit with the verses before and after it?

What is the Holy Spirit intending to communicate through this text?

A P P L Y what God is saying in these verses to your life.

What does this mean today?

What is God saying to you personally?

How can you apply this message to your life?

R E S P O N D to what you've read.

In what ways does this passage call you to action?

How will you be different because of what you've learned?

Write out a prayer to God in response to what you read today:

157//MATTHEW 5

MEMORY VERSES: MATTHEW 5:16; MATTHEW 6:33

After Jesus' time in the desert, He launched into His public ministry by proclaiming the message that the kingdom of God was at hand, choosing His disciples, and preaching to and healing the crowds. With Matthew 5, the Gospel shifts to the record of Jesus' Sermon on the Mount—His teaching on how citizens of the kingdom of God should conduct themselves. The sermon begins with the Beatitudes, blessings God gives to people who cultivate certain spiritual attributes. They emphasize inner motives rather than mere outward conformity. Jesus then shifted His message to the issue of behavior. Jesus addressed several Jewish laws and helped His disciples understand how right behavior is never the ultimate indicator. A person must have the right heart motive too. The commands of God remind us that He has a plan for how we ought to live our lives, and that plan is based in who He is and how He's treated us. Ultimately, we must remember that the God who demands perfection has already provided a means through the perfect sacrifice of His Son, Jesus.

H

E

A

R

158//MATTHEW 6

MEMORY VERSES: MATTHEW 5:16; MATTHEW 6:33

As Jesus continued His Sermon on the Mount, He taught that religious behaviors—specifically giving, praying, and fasting—can be carried out through healthy or unhealthy motives. The inappropriate motive focuses on recognition and attention, while the appropriate motive is aimed at sacrifice and worship of God. Included in this teaching is Jesus' well-known "model prayer," which highlights prayer as a means of worshiping God, aligning ourselves with His will, and depending on Him to meet our daily physical and spiritual needs. The rest of Matthew 6 addresses our priorities from a Kingdom perspective. Jesus was particularly concerned with showing how anxiety and worry can prevent us from receiving the full benefit of God's blessing. This is important because our priorities get the bulk of our time and attention, and they reveal our level of trust in God. Kingdom people should aspire to a singular focus on God and a loyalty to Him. Worry is the opposite of trust in God.

H

E

A

R

159//MATTHEW 7

MEMORY VERSES: MATTHEW 5:16; MATTHEW 6:33

Relationships are the focus of the next section of the Sermon on the Mount. Jesus teaches that His kingdom people are not to be judgmental and condemning of others. The loving relationship we enjoy with God sets the standard for our relationships with others. Jesus also taught that prayer is the primary way we function in relationship with God, and He wants us to continually approach Him with our requests. He delights to give us what we need. Jesus specifically teaches that our prayers are powerful when we are persistent, when we believe God's promise, and when we trust God's heart. Jesus' sermon builds to a climactic ending in chapter 7, when He challenged His listeners to make a choice—would they follow Him through the narrow gate into the Kingdom, or would they choose the wide gate that leads to ultimate destruction? The true Christian is marked by obedience that flows from a real, personal relationship with Jesus Christ.

H

E

A

R

160//MATTHEW 8

MEMORY VERSES: MATTHEW 5:16; MATTHEW 6:33

After the Sermon on the Mount, Matthew's Gospel returns to Jesus' ministry, which was marked by miraculous healings and wonders. Matthew 8 records three miracles of healing that demonstrated slightly different aspects of Jesus' power. The cleansing of the leper demonstrated Jesus' power over one of the worst diseases of the day. The healing of the centurion's servant showed that Jesus did not need to be physically present to heal. At Capernaum, Jesus cast out demons, which demonstrated His sovereign power over evil. After those healings, Jesus illustrated the true nature of discipleship. True discipleship is defined by trust in Jesus, no matter what the circumstances may be. The next two miracles, the calming of the storm and the two men possessed by multiple demons, demonstrate Jesus' power over nature itself and over the most extensive and entrenched evil. The complete picture of Jesus' power on display in Matthew 8 shows that, through Christ, the God of the universe transforms individual lives.

H

E

A

R

161//LUKE 9:10-62

MEMORY VERSES: LUKE 14:26-27; LUKE 14:33

Luke 9 is one of the most important chapters of Scripture related to understanding what it means to be a disciple of Jesus. It includes teachings and miracles from Jesus that provide instruction and demonstration of His ministry in action. Jesus showed His concern for people's physical needs when He fed the hungry crowd. He displayed His power over evil by healing a boy from demon possession. Through Jesus' conversations with His disciples, we learn about His true identity and mission as the Son of God, who would die and be resurrected as the atonement for sin. Jesus' transfiguration with Moses and Elijah validated God's approval of His Son and the mission He was living out. As Jesus' disciples, we are challenged to live in service to others. Jesus did not sugarcoat discipleship; instead, He taught that following Him is about putting the needs of others—both physical and spiritual—ahead of our own.

As you read the Bible this week...

HIGHLIGHT the verses that speak to you.

Write out the name of the book:

Which chapter and verse numbers stand out to you?

EXPLAIN what this passage means.

To whom was it originally written? Why?

How does it fit with the verses before and after it?

What is the Holy Spirit intending to communicate through this text?

APPLY what God is saying in these verses to your life.

What does this mean today?

What is God saying to you personally?

How can you apply this message to your life?

RESPOND to what you've read.

In what ways does this passage call you to action?

How will you be different because of what you've learned?

Write out a prayer to God in response to what you read today:

162//MARK 9

MEMORY VERSES: LUKE 14:26-27; LUKE 14:33

After Jesus' prediction of His suffering, death, and resurrection and His rebuke of Peter, Jesus spoke about the duty of those who follow Him. Before the glory of salvation comes suffering. Because of the great level of sacrifice required, it is important that we understand who Jesus is, which was the very point of His transfiguration. On a high mountain, Jesus was transformed in the midst of Peter, James, and John. Elijah and Moses joined Him. Jesus used this event to inform the disciples further about His coming death and victorious resurrection. As soon as they came down from the mountain, these men were reminded of the importance of faith in God as the foundation for ministry. A desperate father asked the disciples to cast a demon out of his deaf and mute son. They tried and failed. When Jesus discovered their inability to cast out the demon, He attributed it to a lack of faith on their part. By contrast, the father displayed faith as He trusted Jesus to heal the boy. No matter what Jesus calls you to do and what sacrifice is required as His disciple, the most important thing is that you put your faith and trust in Him as you live out that call.

H

E

A

R

163//LUKE 12

MEMORY VERSES: LUKE 14:26-27; LUKE 14:33

Throughout Jesus' earthly ministry, He taught His followers truths to live by. Among the practical teachings in Luke 12, Jesus encouraged His followers to avoid hypocrisy by revering God and by boldly confessing Jesus before others. He also told a parable to warn them about greed and worry. The life of a child of God should be one marked by trust in Him as the ultimate Provider and Protector. Throughout Scripture, God proves that He takes care of His children. He also reminds us that this world is not our home, so the temporary things wrapped up in it should not lead to fear or worry. The temporary nature of this world is the point of Jesus' parable on expectantly awaiting the Master's return. For the disciple of Jesus, this world is about anticipating and preparing for eternity. Our emphasis in the meantime should be on a life of obedience to Christ and participation in His gospel ministry.

H

E

A

R

164//JOHN 3—4

MEMORY VERSES: LUKE 14:26-27; LUKE 14:33

John 3 and 4 include two important conversations Jesus had with two very different individuals—a Pharisee named Nicodemus and a Samaritan woman. Jesus' conversation with Nicodemus (John 3) sheds light on what is required to become a part of the kingdom of God, which takes place through a relationship with Jesus. At the heart of Jesus' teaching is the concept of being "born again," which speaks to the life-changing effect of the Holy Spirit in a person's life. This change takes place as a person confesses that Jesus is the Son of God, who died to pay the price for his or her sins. That confession makes way for the forgiving power of God's grace. In John 4, Jesus described the new life available in Him as "living water" in His conversation with the woman at the well. The idea of living water that forever satisfies a person's thirst speaks to eternal life with God—one of the benefits of salvation from sin through Jesus. Both of these conversations give us insight into salvation and the benefits it brings, and both remind us that Jesus is central to salvation. Only a relationship with Him brings the spiritual satisfaction and fulfillment we desire.

H

E

A

R

165//LUKE 14

MEMORY VERSES: LUKE 14:26-27; LUKE 14:33

In Luke 14, Jesus told two parables in a banquet setting to teach the need for humility. Through these parables, we learn that God values and honors a humble spirit that seeks to put others ahead of oneself. This is the very example Jesus modeled for us. He left His position with God the Father in heaven and came to earth in order to make a way for sinful humanity to be reunited with God. His actions required humility on many levels, culminating at the cross, where the very Son of God died for us. Jesus is our model for a life of humble service in the kingdom of God. A third parable about a king going to battle anticipated disciples counting the cost before following Jesus. In order to be obedient to Jesus' call to discipleship, we must prioritize Him and His mission above everything else in life—even above life itself.

H

E

A

R

166 //JOHN 6

MEMORY VERSES: MARK 10:45; JOHN 6:37

While there are many points of similarity between the four Gospels, there are also considerable differences. Each writer had a unique message he wanted to communicate to a particular audience. Among the teachings unique to John's Gospel are the "I Am" statements of Jesus. With each of these, Jesus reveals His attributes. In John 6 Jesus said, "I am the bread of life." He declared this immediately after miraculously feeding a large crowd. By meeting the people's physical need for food and then declaring Himself to be the Bread of Life, Jesus helps us see that He alone can satisfy our spiritual hunger. Everyone is born with spiritual hunger, whether they recognize it or not, and people attempt to supplement many things to fill this spiritual void, including religion, materialism, and relationships. But the only thing capable of satisfying a person's spiritual hunger is to know Jesus as his or her loving Savior.

As you read the Bible this week...

HIGHLIGHT the verses that speak to you.

Write out the name of the book:

Which chapter and verse numbers stand out to you?

EXPLAIN what this passage means.

To whom was it originally written? Why?

How does it fit with the verses before and after it?

What is the Holy Spirit intending to communicate through this text?

APPLY what God is saying in these verses to your life.

What does this mean today?

What is God saying to you personally?

How can you apply this message to your life?

RESPOND to what you've read.

In what ways does this passage call you to action?

How will you be different because of what you've learned?

Write out a prayer to God in response to what you read today:

167//MATTHEW 19:16-30

MEMORY VERSES: MARK 10:45; JOHN 6:37

Matthew 19:16-30 tells about Jesus' conversation with a man known only as the rich young ruler. This man approached Jesus during a time when He was teaching and asked about the necessary requirements for eternal life with God. In response, Jesus told the man to sell all of his possessions and give the money to the poor. Although the man was faithful to obey the law, he refused to give up everything to follow Jesus. Jesus' instruction to this man highlighted the idols in his life—his money and possessions mattered greatly to him. They were his whole identity. However, Jesus teaches time and again that nothing can have a greater priority in our lives than following Jesus, and our faith in God should be the source of our identity. Through His conversation with the rich young ruler, Jesus revealed that He knows our hearts, and He knows what we are tempted to place above Him.

H

E

A

R

168//LUKE 15–16

MEMORY VERSES: MARK 10:45; JOHN 6:37

In Luke 15-16, Jesus used a series of parables (an illustrative story used to communicate spiritual truth) to teach His listeners important lessons about His relationship with us and how we are to live in response to Him. The three parables in Luke 15, often referred to as the "Lost Parables," describe the joy associated with the repentance of sinners. All of heaven rejoices when people turn to God through faith in Jesus. These parables remind us that all people matter to God and that their salvation should matter to us too. As the parable of the prodigal son demonstrates, no sin is so great that it can keep us out of reach of God's loving grace. Once we experience salvation, everything changes, including how we live day to day and how we view the things of this world. That new perspective is central to the parables and teachings in Luke 16, which have to do with handling money. In the kingdom of God, money can serve a good purpose when used properly. When viewed from the wrong perspective, however, money can blind a person from what matters most—a right relationship with God.

H

E

A

R

169//LUKE 17:11-37; 18

MEMORY VERSES: MARK 10:45; JOHN 6:37

One of the themes that surfaces in the Gospels is that salvation changes us. One of the stories in Luke 10 tells about ten lepers who were healed by Jesus. Of the ten, only one returned to thank Him, but that one revealed the truth of how understanding the change Jesus has brought about in our lives should lead to a heart of gratitude toward Him. Prayer also played a significant role in Jesus' life and teaching. At the start of Luke 18, we read a story Jesus told about a widow, which highlights the need for persistence in prayer even when it seems like God is being slow to answer (2 Pet. 3:9). A second parable about the Pharisee and the tax collector emphasizes the need for humility in prayer. Both persistence and humility in prayer communicate total dependency on God and a desire to spend time with Him. Prayer is one of the greatest gifts God gives His children and is a gift for which we, like the leper, should be eternally grateful.

H

E

A

R

170//MARK 10

MEMORY VERSES: MARK 10:45; JOHN 6:37

Many times during His earthly ministry, Jesus predicted His own death and the suffering His disciples would endure. He wanted those who followed Him to have a clear picture of what they were getting themselves into—connecting with the mission of Jesus requires sacrifice. Contrary to how the disciples viewed it, Jesus defined effective discipleship by the act of humbly serving other people (Mark 10:42-45). He downplayed success as gained through position and power. Real effectiveness in ministry comes through serving, not through being served. This mindset was counter cultural in Jesus' day, and it remains counter cultural today too. Serving others requires paying attention to people's needs and a genuine compassion for people's souls. When we struggle to show this kind of humility and compassion to others, it is important to remember that this is how God loves us. Recognizing the love, compassion, and grace of God in our own lives enables us to share that love with others.

H

E

A

R

171//JOHN 11; MATTHEW 21:1-13

MEMORY VERSES: JOHN 13:34-35; JOHN 15:4-5

John 11 records one of Jesus' greatest miracles. Lazarus, the brother of Mary and Martha, featured prominently in Jesus' life and ministry, died and was buried before Jesus arrived to heal him. However, Lazarus' death gave Jesus the opportunity to show that He even has authority over death, something only God Himself can claim. Another of the "I Am" statements in John's Gospel is found in this account—Jesus said, "I am the resurrection and the life." This means that eternal life with God is possible only through a relationship with Jesus. After this miracle, the threat against Jesus' life intensified. Matthew 21:1-13 describes Jesus' triumphal entry into Jerusalem and the cleansing of the temple, which further testified to His authority and identity as the Messiah, the promised Son of God. The triumphal entry also marked the beginning of the end of Jesus' earthly ministry, as His death on the cross loomed near.

As you read the Bible this week...

HIGHLIGHT the verses that speak to you.

Write out the name of the book:

Which chapter and verse numbers stand out to you?

EXPLAIN what this passage means.

To whom was it originally written? Why?

How does it fit with the verses before and after it?

What is the Holy Spirit intending to communicate through this text?

APPLY what God is saying in these verses to your life.

What does this mean today?

What is God saying to you personally?

How can you apply this message to your life?

RESPOND to what you've read.

In what ways does this passage call you to action?

How will you be different because of what you've learned?

Write out a prayer to God in response to what you read today:

172//JOHN 13

Jesus' sacrificial death occupies a central focus in John's Gospel, as everything moves toward a climax at the cross and a triumph through the resurrection. The first 12 chapters of John's Gospel focus on Jesus' life, teachings, and ministry. With chapter 13, the focus shifts to His final meal with His disciples before His arrest, death, resurrection, and His appearances to believers. At this moment in Jesus' ministry, He turned His attention to His disciples both to prepare them for the coming events and to teach them the Kingdom qualities of humility, service, and love. In spite of His knowledge about Judas' betrayal, Peter's denial, and the general unfaithfulness of the disciples, Jesus demonstrated a servant attitude toward His disciples on the evening prior to His arrest. He washed His disciples' feet and utilized that experience as a time to teach His disciples about loving and humble service. Even today, Jesus continues to call His followers to imitate His example, even when serving is uncomfortable and inconvenient.

H

E

A

R

173//JOHN 14–15

After Jesus washed the disciples' feet, He continued to outline expectations for each of them after His death. Anticipating the sorrow His disciples would experience at His departure, Jesus offered a message of comfort and consolation to enable them to live confidently. In another of Jesus' "I Am" statements, He referred to Himself as "the way, and the truth, and the life." Apart from Jesus, there is no means of knowing God and no hope of abundant, eternal life. One more "I Am" statement is found in John 15, when Jesus said, "I am the true vine." The imagery of this chapter describes Jesus' relationship with believers in two ways: (1) vine and branches and (2) master and friends. As branches, we have the responsibility of abiding in Him so we can experience a productive life. As friends, we have the privilege of understanding His mission for us and through us as we obey His commands.

H

E

A

R

174//JOHN 16

MEMORY VERSES: JOHN 13:34-35; JOHN 15:4-5

In the final instructions given to His disciples in the upper room on the night before His crucifixion (John 13–16), Jesus promised that He would ask the Father to send the Holy Spirit to His disciples (14:15-17). He revealed that the Holy Spirit would be their Counselor (14:25-26). The Holy Spirit would testify about Jesus Christ and enable believers to testify also (15:26-27). The Spirit's ministry to the world would be to convict people of sin and bring them to faith and salvation in Jesus Christ (16:5-15). The Holy Spirit would guide believers into all truth. Genuine spirituality involves growing in a personal knowledge of and experience with the person and ministry of the Holy Spirit in our daily lives. Only through the Spirit's strength are we able to find the hope and confidence Jesus encourages at the close of this chapter with the words, "Take heart; I have overcome the world" (John 16:33, ESV).

H

E

A

R

175//MATTHEW 24:1-31

MEMORY VERSES: JOHN 13:34-35; JOHN 15:4-5

Matthew 24 contains several teachings from Jesus concerning the future. As His death drew closer, Jesus knew the disciples needed to be prepared for the suffering and persecution that would eventually come, and He also knew they needed a reason to maintain hope when things grew challenging. Jesus prophesied about the fall of the temple, which took place in the year A.D. 70. To the disciples' question concerning signs of the end, Jesus replied that we should not misinterpret the signs. Persecutions of various types are to be expected. False messiahs will arise. People will be deceived. All of these things will take place before Jesus Himself will return and right the world once and for all. It can be hard to process teachings like these from Jesus because the final days come with so much uncertainty, but the most important takeaway is that Jesus will return again. We must be ready when He does.

H

E

A

R

176//MATTHEW 24:32-51

MEMORY VERSES: LUKE 23:34; JOHN 17:3

One of the things Scripture teaches us is that the end times will be a time of judgment. This is good news for people who know Jesus as their Savior and Lord, but it is bad news for people who do not have a personal relationship with Him. In Matthew 24, Jesus illustrated the certainty of judgment with the parable of the fig tree and warned against trying to predict the time of His return. The real need is not for insight to read the times, but perseverance to remain faithful and dedication to the mission of bringing more people to Christ. While we wait for Jesus to return, we must share the gospel so that as many people as possible can have the hope and promise of eternal life with Jesus.

As you read the Bible this week...

HIGHLIGHT the verses that speak to you.

Write out the name of the book:

Which chapter and verse numbers stand out to you?

EXPLAIN what this passage means.

To whom was it originally written? Why?

How does it fit with the verses before and after it?

What is the Holy Spirit intending to communicate through this text?

APPLY what God is saying in these verses to your life.

What does this mean today?

What is God saying to you personally?

How can you apply this message to your life?

RESPOND to what you've read.

In what ways does this passage call you to action?

How will you be different because of what you've learned?

Write out a prayer to God in response to what you read today:

177///JOHN 17

MEMORY VERSES: LUKE 23:34; JOHN 17:3

John 17 is referred to as Jesus' "High Priestly Prayer." Jesus' prayer on the eve of His arrest and trials includes a prayer for Himself, a prayer for His disciples, and a prayer for future believers of every age. Jesus' prayer for Himself was that He would glorify His Father through His death. He then prayed that His disciples would glorify the Father by preserving the unity they had in Jesus. Within this section of the prayer, Jesus petitioned the Father to protect His disciples from the Evil One. Finally, Jesus prayed for all who would come to believe in Him in the future. He wanted these believers to experience unity and grow in knowledge and love. By demonstrating unity, unbelievers would respond to the message of the gospel while believers glorify the Father. Jesus' selfless prayer is a model for all of us.

H

E

A

R

178//MATTHEW 26:35–27:31

After Jesus finished the Passover meal and wrapped up His teachings, the events of the crucifixion night were set in motion. While Jesus retreated to pray, Judas—one of Jesus' own disciples—showed up with an army of people to arrest Him. Jesus was immediately taken to trial before the high priest. Chapter 26 ends with Jesus being condemned by the Sanhedrin and Peter denying that he even knew Him. Matthew concentrates on Jesus' trial and death. Through injustice and persecution, Jesus remained humble and steadfast in His obedience to the will of the Father. Jesus' interrogation ends with Pilate granting the religious leaders' request to sentence Jesus to crucifixion in place of Barabbas, a guilty criminal. With that verdict, Jesus in His innocence was delivered over to death, just as was prophesied. We are all like Barabbas—sinful people who stand guilty before God, but for whom Jesus gave His life in order to pay the price that our sinfulness demands. Because He died, we can live.

H

E

A

R

179//MATTHEW 27:32-66; LUKE 23:26-56

MEMORY VERSES: LUKE 23:34; JOHN 17:3

Today's readings from Matthew and Luke give the account of Jesus' death on the cross, the event up to which His entire ministry had been leading. Crucifixion was the most painful and barbaric form of capital punishment in ancient times. The Romans at first used it only for slaves, then later for enemies of the state, and by the first century as a way to discourage criminal activity. Jesus was none of these. However, His sacrificial death was always God's plan. Jesus' crucifixion produced different responses from those who saw it. One of the two criminals crucified alongside Jesus insulted Him, while the other asked His forgiveness. The religious leaders and soldiers mocked Him. A centurion confessed Jesus' righteous nature. Among the Gospel writers, only Luke reported Jesus' prayer of forgiveness on the cross. Forgiveness is a key tenet of the message Jesus would instruct His followers to proclaim in His name to all nations following His resurrection. Jesus' death proved His ministry of reconciliation, hope, and healing to be the truth.

H

E

A

R

180//JOHN 19

MEMORY VERSES: LUKE 23:34; JOHN 17:3

In chapter 18, John described Jesus' arrest and trials before the high priest and before Pilate. Pilate found no basis for the charges against Jesus, but he wasn't willing to sacrifice himself and his own political interests to set Christ free. Therefore, he caved to the religious leaders' demands for Jesus' death. Though Pilate handed Jesus over to the Jews to be crucified, it is important to note that Jesus willingly gave Himself to die a sacrificial death for the sins of the world. He gave Himself so that we could receive salvation through Him. Jesus' death occurred at the season of the Passover celebration. He died as the Lamb of God (John 1:29,36). The blood of the lambs sprinkled on their homes in obedience to God's command had spared the Israelites when the destroyer invaded the land of Egypt before the Israelites left for the promised land (Ex. 12:13). John wrote in 1 John 1:7 that "the blood of Jesus His Son cleanses us from all sin." Jesus died for us.

H

E

A

R

181//MARK 16

MEMORY VERSES: MATTHEW 28:18-20; ACTS 1:8

All of Scripture points to the work and mission of Jesus, which seemed to end the day He hung on the cross. At least, that's how things appeared to His disciples. Little did they know the cross was only part one of Jesus' redemptive act. With His death, Jesus paid God's penalty for the sins of the world. On the third day, He rose from the grave and defeated death—the ultimate consequence of sin. Mark documents the moment three of Jesus' faithful followers, all women, showed up at His tomb to anoint His body. They encountered an angel who told them of Jesus' resurrection. The angel also told them to take this news to the disciples and Peter. God wanted this great news conveyed as an offer of restoration and forgiveness. Through the cross and resurrection of Jesus, God made a way for you—a sinful and broken son or daughter—to be reunited with Him as the recipient of His forgiveness and grace.

As you read the Bible this week...

HIGHLIGHT the verses that speak to you.

Write out the name of the book:

Which chapter and verse numbers stand out to you?

EXPLAIN what this passage means.

To whom was it originally written? Why?

How does it fit with the verses before and after it?

What is the Holy Spirit intending to communicate through this text?

APPLY what God is saying in these verses to your life.

What does this mean today?

What is God saying to you personally?

How can you apply this message to your life?

RESPOND to what you've read.

In what ways does this passage call you to action?

How will you be different because of what you've learned?

Write out a prayer to God in response to what you read today:

182//LUKE 24

MEMORY VERSES: MATTHEW 28:18-20; ACTS 1:8

The Gospel of Luke also records Jesus' resurrection and the women's faithful obedience in relaying the angel's message to the rest of the disciples. Luke also gives us details into Jesus' post-resurrection appearances, which proved His resurrection and provided Him the opportunity to give final charges to His disciples before ascending to heaven. Jesus appeared to two disciples on the road to Emmaus, when He also confirmed that all of Scripture points to Himself. Jesus later appeared to the apostles and showed them His hands and feet. He prompted them to believe the resurrection by eating with them and interpreting the Old Testament in light of His sufferings and resurrection. Jesus identified Himself as the Messiah. His time on earth ended with a commission to His disciples. He left them with the charge to minister and proclaim the gospel on Jesus' behalf. As Jesus' disciples today, we know Him because others have been faithful to carry His gospel around the world, and we pick up where those disciples left off as Jesus' faithful ambassadors.

H

E

A

R

183//JOHN 20–21

In John's Gospel account of Jesus' resurrection, John zooms in on specific conversations Jesus had with His disciples after His resurrection. We see how their faith was impacted by His resurrection, and as a result, how ours should be too. The evening after Mary discovered the empty tomb, Jesus appeared to His disciples who were huddled behind locked doors. Jesus appeared a week later to the disciples, including Thomas, who had difficult time believing the news since he was absent during His first encounter. Jesus invited Thomas to see and touch His scars. Thomas responded in faith without touching His wounds. Jesus' final appearance was to Peter and six other disciples on the seashore as they were fishing. During that time, Jesus commissioned Peter to follow Him and minister to His people. Jesus' conversation with Peter demonstrates that love was essential for being a faithful disciple. Believers exemplify love for Jesus by caring for His people. If we really love Jesus, we will serve Him by caring for other believers.

H

E

A

R

184//MATTHEW 28

MEMORY VERSES: MATTHEW 28:18-20; ACTS 1:8

The record of the resurrection is surprisingly short in all of the Gospels. The writers were not necessarily trying to prove the resurrection because it was considered largely indisputable in the early church. They were satisfied with sharing only a few of His appearances. What Matthew recorded is particularly significant for the assignment Jesus has given to all of His disciples throughout history. Matthew included Jesus' appearance to the women who found the tomb and His appearance to the eleven remaining disciples. It was then that Jesus gave the "Great Commission," His command for the disciples to continue His ministry by making disciples. Sharing Christ and bringing people to God is an ongoing lifestyle commitment, and one that should be lived out with the same sense of urgency the first disciples had. As we continue to live out the Great Commission today, we must remember we are not working in our own strength. Our task is not to be clever, motivational, or exciting. We are to be obedient—humbly claiming the promise that Jesus is with us always.

H

E

A

R

185//ACTS 1

MEMORY VERSES: MATTHEW 28:18-20; ACTS 1:8

The Book of Acts, written by the Gospel writer Luke, documents the early church during the first three decades after Jesus' ascension. Throughout those years, Christianity, which was first extended to the Jewish people, became predominantly Gentile. Acts 1 sets the stage for the coming of the Holy Spirit, which is described in Acts 2, by moving readers from Jesus' post-resurrection appearances to the disciples prayerfully waiting in the upper room. Luke recorded Jesus' instructions to the disciples concerning their global mission, a task that would be aided by the Holy Spirit. Luke also includes the account of Jesus' ascension to heaven as the disciples watched. As Jesus prepared to leave, He gave the disciples a new perspective about the Kingdom when He established a worldwide scope for this witnessing mission. The Church, under the Holy Spirit's guidance and power, was to take the gospel to the ends of the earth, a task that we are charged with continuing to carry out today.

H

E

A

R

186//ACTS 2–3

MEMORY VERSES: ACTS 2:42; ACTS 4:31

As Jesus had promised, the Father empowered the disciples with the Holy Spirit. We have been commissioned to witness about Christ to the world and are dependent on the Spirit's power to accomplish this. Chapter 2 ends with the crowd's response to Peter's sermon. Having come under conviction by the Holy Spirit, the people want to know how to respond. Peter directs them to confess and repent of their sins. Chapters 2 and 3 provide a picture of the church in action. Unity, generous giving, sharing with those in need, witnessing, worshiping, partaking of the Lord's Supper in fellowship, and serving the Lord present a model for ministry. Following Jesus' example, the disciples met people's physical and spiritual needs. Just as He did in the first century, God continues to empower His people to meet the spiritual and physical needs of others in order that His name would be glorified and people would be drawn to Him.

As you read the Bible this week...

H I G H L I G H T the verses that speak to you.

Write out the name of the book:

Which chapter and verse numbers stand out to you?

E X P L A I N what this passage means.

To whom was it originally written? Why?

How does it fit with the verses before and after it?

What is the Holy Spirit intending to communicate through this text?

A P P L Y what God is saying in these verses to your life.

What does this mean today?

What is God saying to you personally?

How can you apply this message to your life?

R E S P O N D to what you've read.

In what ways does this passage call you to action?

How will you be different because of what you've learned?

Write out a prayer to God in response to what you read today:

187//ACTS 4–5

MEMORY VERSES: ACTS 2:42; ACTS 4:31

The early church experienced many miraculous signs and wonders as a result of their unity with others and dependence upon the Spirit. Acts 4:32-37 describes how early believers shared their possessions for the purpose of meeting physical needs. Barnabas exemplified voluntary sharing among the believers. Sadly, not every member possessed pure motives. Ananias and Sapphira were dishonest about their personal contribution and, as a result, experienced the harsh judgment of death. Ananias and Sapphira remind us that the church is made up of imperfect people trying to meet the needs of others and bring people to Jesus. This is why dependence on the wisdom and guidance of the Holy Spirit in daily life is vitally important. When we don't listen to the Spirit, we are tempted to imitate the actions of Ananias and Sapphira, who misled the disciples. But because God always accomplishes His good plans in our world, this event served to enhance the church's public ministry. People were encouraged to seek out the church's assistance, which led to conversations about the One who could satisfy every need.

H

E

A

R

188//ACTS 6

As the church continued to grow at a rapid pace, noticeable growing pains began to surface. In chapter 6, Luke described how some widows in the Christian community in Jerusalem were not receiving their daily distribution of food. This brought to the church's attention the need for better administration of service so the apostles could focus on the spread of the gospel. The church set apart seven men to head up this new ministry. As the gospel went forth, opposition against the church increased. Stephen, one of the seven men appointed to serve the widows, drew attention from the corrupt religious leaders because of his fearless proclamation of the Word of Christ. His preaching led some unbelieving Grecian Jews to bring him before the Sanhedrin on trumped-up charges. When the gospel changes lives through a noticeable impact on a community, opposition will arise. All who desire to live out Jesus' Great Commission in their lives can expect hardship and trouble along the way. Like Stephen, though, God's Spirit will give you the boldness and confidence to stand strong for Him.

H
_____

E
_____

_____

_____

A
_____

_____

_____

R
_____

_____

_____

189//ACTS 7

MEMORY VERSES: ACTS 2:42; ACTS 4:31

In Acts 7, Luke records the defense Stephen gave before the Sanhedrin—a powerful testimony of the gospel, traced throughout the Old Testament. Stephen opened with God's calling of Abraham in Mesopotamia. He then highlighted Joseph and his brothers residing in Egypt. Next, Stephen recounted the Israelites' slavery in Egypt and Moses' journey to freedom through the desert. He reminded the crowd of the Israelites' rebellion in the wilderness and how they worshiped an idol. After discussing the traveling tabernacle and the temple of Solomon, Stephen emphasized that God does not dwell in buildings. Stephen boldly warned the religious leaders about "resisting the Holy Spirit." Their ancestors had persecuted and killed the prophets, and now the religious leaders had killed the Righteous One (Jesus), whom the prophets foretold. Stephen's defense was a powerful witness about Christ, which resulted in his death by stoning. He is the first martyr in the New Testament.

H

E

A

R

190//ACTS 8–9

MEMORY VERSES: ACTS 2:42; ACTS 4:31

Stephen's stoning unleashed a persecution on the Jerusalem church that forced believers to flee from Jerusalem. Instead of extinguishing the gospel message, it expanded it. Saul, a persecutor of Christians, who later became known as the apostle Paul, is introduced at the account of Stephen's death. The chapter ends with Philip's one-on-one ministry to the Ethiopian eunuch, highlighting another conversation that reveals God's redemptive plan throughout all of Scripture. Chapter 9 begins with Saul's journey to eliminate all believers of Jesus in the city of Damascus. On the way, Jesus encountered him, causing him to lose his sight. After meeting Ananias in Damascus, the former persecutor regained his sight, was filled with the Holy Spirit, and was eventually baptized. Almost immediately, Paul began proclaiming the gospel. Few encounters in Scripture provide such a powerful picture of the immediate change Jesus brings to a person's life. If you are a Christian, then like Saul you have a powerful testimony of how you have been raised from spiritual death to life through the good news of Christ. Don't ever take that story for granted.

H

E

A

R

191//ACTS 10–11

MEMORY VERSES: JAMES 1:2-4; JAMES 2:17

Through Peter's efforts, people understood that the gospel of Jesus Christ is a message for the whole world. In large part, this revelation took place as a result of Peter's interactions with Cornelius, a Roman centurion who had a vision in which an angel told him to send men to summon Peter. Meanwhile, Peter had a vision in which God commanded him to kill and eat animals Jews considered unclean. When Cornelius' men arrived, the Spirit instructed Peter to accompany them to Caesarea. When he entered Cornelius' house, Peter shared how God had sent him and explained the truth he had learned about not considering anyone common or unclean. Peter preached the gospel at Cornelius' house, the Spirit descended upon the hearers, and they were baptized. In God's kingdom, people are more important than religious regulations or racial differences. God's desire is for all to hear His gospel and experience salvation.

As you read the Bible this week...

HIGHLIGHT the verses that speak to you.

Write out the name of the book:

Which chapter and verse numbers stand out to you?

EXPLAIN what this passage means.

To whom was it originally written? Why?

How does it fit with the verses before and after it?

What is the Holy Spirit intending to communicate through this text?

APPLY what God is saying in these verses to your life.

What does this mean today?

What is God saying to you personally?

How can you apply this message to your life?

RESPOND to what you've read.

In what ways does this passage call you to action?

How will you be different because of what you've learned?

Write out a prayer to God in response to what you read today:

192//ACTS 12

MEMORY VERSES: JAMES 1:2-4; JAMES 2:17

Persecutions against the early church continued, even though Paul was no longer leading the charge. King Herod Agrippa I, ruler of Judea, beheaded the apostle James and imprisoned Peter. Acts 12 described how an angel miraculously freed Peter from prison. Herod discovered that Peter had escaped, had Peter's guards executed, and journeyed to Caesarea. There, Herod suffered a horrible death. In spite of the oppression, the gospel continued to flourish. Additionally, Barnabas and Paul completed their relief mission at this time. It's easy to overlook a small detail in Acts 12:5. While Peter was in prison, the church "earnestly" prayed for him, likely for his safety and strength in the face of persecution. The events that followed show the power of their prayers, which reminds us that prayer is the most effective tool we have against any opposition or temptation we face. Through prayer, we spend time with with God and rely on Him for every aspect of our lives.

H

E

A

R

193//ACTS 13–14

MEMORY VERSES: JAMES 1:2-4; JAMES 2:17

With Acts 13, Luke shifted his focus from Peter to Paul. One of the consistent themes of Paul's missionary efforts was preaching in the synagogue, which he did several times in Acts 13–14. Paul was born and raised as a devout Jew, and conversion of the Jews was at the heart of his ministry. However, most Jews were not receptive to Paul's gospel message; therefore, he took the message to the Gentiles. Paul's preaching always included that Jesus was the Son of God who was crucified, raised from death, and the means through which people can receive forgiveness of sins and be made right with God. This message stirred people's hearts both to belief and to anger. Those Paul angered often tried to kill him, as is evident from Acts 13–14, though these threats on his life never hindered Paul's witness. Through Paul's example, we are reminded that serving Christ brings with it both highs and lows. Regardless of what we encounter as we live for Christ, God expects us to be faithful to the task He has given us.

H

E

A

R

194//JAMES 1–2

Acts 12:17 identified James, the brother of Jesus, as a leader of the church in Jerusalem. The Book of James is a practical book that addresses issues Christians deal with both within and outside of the church. In chapter 1, James reminded his readers that God offers believers wisdom to cope with times of trials and testing. He pointed out that God never tempts anyone; temptations arise from people's sin natures. God, on the other hand, graciously gives only good gifts to those He loves. James also emphasized the importance of listening to and obeying the Word of God. By applying God's Word, we show others that our religion is genuine. Applying the Word involves controlling our speech, caring for people, and maintaining purity. In chapter 2, James shifted his focus from religion to personal faith. As Christians, we are obligated to love others. We are sinning when we fail to do so. Love is one of the ways we put feet to our faith, which, as James pointed out, is dead without actions. The point James makes in these two chapters is that saving faith in Jesus changes a person from the inside out.

H

E

A

R

195//JAMES 3–5

MEMORY VERSES: JAMES 1:2-4; JAMES 2:17

One of the running themes throughout James' letter is right Christian behavior. As people transformed by Jesus, Christians are to live and act differently than the rest of the world. Paul specifically connected this to speech. James emphasized the power of our words—either for good or for bad—and the need for consistency in believers' speech. James also reminded his readers that Christians must rely on the wisdom of God to control their behavior. In addition to speech, James warned against the danger of unaddressed conflict. Evidently, judging others was a significant problem in the early church, which fueled conflicts. James stressed the availability of God's grace to correct believers' conflicts with one another. On the basis of that grace, he called on them to submit and draw near to God through repentance and humility. After some additional teachings, James closed his letter by calling for believers to be patient through suffering as they await Jesus' return and to endure on the basis of God's nature. In the meantime, we are to maintain our faith in God and utilize the power of prayer He has given us.

H

E

A

R

196//ACTS 15–16

MEMORY VERSES: ACTS 17:11; ACTS 17:24-25

As the church grew, so did the need for clarity between Jewish and Christian beliefs. Paul and Barnabas met with the council at Jerusalem to discuss the role of Old Testament Law in the life of new believers. Peter declared Jews were saved by grace just as Gentiles were. Paul, Barnabas, and James affirmed God's intention that Gentiles be included in His family. James concluded that believers should not demand Gentiles become Jewish converts in order to become Christians. Following the council, Paul began his second missionary journey, traveling to Philippi where Lydia and her household became believers. Exorcising a fortune-telling spirit from a girl resulted in their imprisonment. An earthquake opened the jail's doors, but no prisoners escaped. Paul and Silas shared Christ with the jailer, and he and his household became believers. Because of Paul's Roman citizenship, the missionaries were freed and resumed their journey.

As you read the Bible this week...

HIGHLIGHT the verses that speak to you.

Write out the name of the book:

Which chapter and verse numbers stand out to you?

EXPLAIN what this passage means.

To whom was it originally written? Why?

How does it fit with the verses before and after it?

What is the Holy Spirit intending to communicate through this text?

APPLY what God is saying in these verses to your life.

What does this mean today?

What is God saying to you personally?

How can you apply this message to your life?

RESPOND to what you've read.

In what ways does this passage call you to action?

How will you be different because of what you've learned?

Write out a prayer to God in response to what you read today:

197//GALATIANS 1–3

MEMORY VERSES: ACTS 17:11; ACTS 17:24-25

As with many of his New Testament letters, Paul wrote his letter to the Galatians with a specific purpose and audience in mind. He wrote Galatians to correct their faulty understanding of faith and practice related to the gospel. Like the issue raised at the Jerusalem council, many were Judaizers, which means they believed Gentiles had to be converted to Judaism in order to be Christians. However, as Paul argued in his letter, justification (being made right before God) comes by grace through faith in Christ, not through keeping the Law. Paul contrasted living under the Law to living by faith. The Law fulfilled its purpose in that it acted as a guardian to God's people, protecting them as a foreshadowing or representation of the covering blood of Christ that was to come. It was also a guide to the coming Messiah. When Christ did come, He fulfilled the Law, which means faith in Him is the only thing necessary to experience His saving faith. Obedience to God's Law follows as the way we live out our faith in Him.

H

E

A

R

198//GALATIANS 4–6

MEMORY VERSES: ACTS 17:11; ACTS 17:24-25

In Galatians 4–6, Paul emphasizes the Christian's identity as a child of God. God has adopted believers as His children and given them the Holy Spirit. They are no longer slaves but heirs of God, which is why it's offensive to God when we obey the Law in an attempt to earn His love and grace. Paul emphasized that God's call to salvation in Christ is a call to freedom. This freedom is not license to sin, but liberation to serve others. Loving others fulfills the Law. Infighting among Christians, however, is destructive, as is any item on the list of "the works of the flesh," which Paul mentioned in chapter 5. On the other hand, the Spirit's activity in Christians produces a cluster of virtues—the fruit of the Spirit—which provides evidence that a person belongs to Christ. As those in Christ, we have the responsibility to help bear one another's burdens and do good to others. The point Paul makes repeatedly in Galatians is that true spiritual transformation only comes through the gospel.

H

E

A

R

199//ACTS 17–18:17

MEMORY VERSES: ACTS 17:11; ACTS 17:24-25

Acts 17 documents Paul's ministry in Thessalonica, a place where the gospel was well received. Not surprisingly, jealous Jews forced them on to Berea, where many accepted their message of Christ. Again Jews from Thessalonica caused trouble, so Paul embarked on a journey to Athens. During his stay, he presented the gospel to Jews and Gentiles, some of which put their faith in Jesus. From Athens, Paul traveled to Corinth, where he befriended Priscilla and Aquila, who made a living as tentmakers. When Jews in the synagogue rejected him, he took the message to the Gentiles. For 18 months, Paul taught the Word of God in a house. Antagonistic Jews accused Paul of breaking the Law, but Gallio, the proconsul, dismissed the charges. From this time in Paul's ministry, God's hand was on him. His commitment to the gospel is evidence of this. Like Paul, we need to trust God's leadership in our lives as we live out the calling He has given us to go and make disciples.

H

E

A

R

200//1 THESSALONIANS 1–2

MEMORY VERSES: ACTS 17:11; ACTS 17:24-25

During his time in Thessalonica, Paul formed a strong bond with the Christians there. The new believers had embraced the gospel enthusiastically and formed a church, but because of Paul's abrupt departure, the believers were immature in the faith. Paul did, however, remind them of key events in their lives as believers. Paul thanked God for the transformation he witnessed in their lives as a result of embracing the gospel. They were outstanding examples for other Christians, both near and far. In chapter 2, Paul reminded them about the purpose of his ministry while he lived among them. We look to the apostle Paul as the foremost example of what Christians are to believe and how we are to behave as we seek to grow in Christlikeness. Throughout his life and ministry, Paul placed an emphasis on loving others and sharing the gospel boldly. As Paul demonstrated, we are to live in such a way that both our words and actions draw people to the saving grace and transforming love of God.

H

E

A

R

201//1 THESSALONIANS 3–5

MEMORY VERSES: 1 CORINTHIANS 1:18; 1 THESSALONIANS 5:23-24

Paul devoted the first half of his letter to compliment the Thessalonian Christians on their actions and remind them of his expectations. In chapter 3, he focuses on application of the gospel. Paul essentially asked them to "keep on keeping on." Everything they did was to be driven by the goal of pleasing God. These instructions also included teaching about Jesus' second coming. We all have unanswerable questions about Jesus' return, but what is important to remember is that Jesus' promised return is to be a source of hope, comfort, and motivation. While we wait for Jesus to return, we are to be united with other believers who are striving for Christlikeness with us. For believers, faith (toward God) and love (toward one another) are nothing new. These attitudes are to characterize the Christian life. An ongoing challenge is to show that we are living in anticipation of Jesus' return through behavior distinguished by love, faith, and hope.

As you read the Bible this week...

HIGHLIGHT the verses that speak to you.

Write out the name of the book:

Which chapter and verse numbers stand out to you?

EXPLAIN what this passage means.

To whom was it originally written? Why?

How does it fit with the verses before and after it?

What is the Holy Spirit intending to communicate through this text?

APPLY what God is saying in these verses to your life.

What does this mean today?

What is God saying to you personally?

How can you apply this message to your life?

RESPOND to what you've read.

In what ways does this passage call you to action?

How will you be different because of what you've learned?

Write out a prayer to God in response to what you read today:

202//2 THESSALONIANS 1–3

MEMORY VERSES: 1 CORINTHIANS 1:18; 1 THESSALONIANS 5:23-24

Shortly after Paul had sent his first letter to this group of new believers, he received a report about issues confronting them, prompting him to send them a follow-up letter. Their questions were of Jesus' second coming, an event Paul had touched on briefly in his first letter. Paul instructed them to wait and watch for Jesus' return and not fall prey to false teachers around them. Each chapter of Paul's second letter emphasizes God's sovereignty in a variety of situations. Paul pointed them to God's justice, both now and in the future, which enables believers to feel safe despite troubling circumstances. Paul closed his letter to the church at Thessalonica by encouraging members to hold one another accountable and encourage one another in their pursuits of Jesus. We can endure together because God has proven His faithfulness to us through the life, death, and resurrection of Jesus. Through Jesus, we can hold on to the promise God has given us of eternal life with Him.

H

E

A

R

203//ACTS 18:18–19:41

MEMORY VERSES: 1 CORINTHIANS 1:18; 1 THESSALONIANS 5:23-24

After Paul's time in Thessalonica and Athens, he traveled on to Corinth and then later to Ephesus. In both cities he preached first in the Jewish synagogue until he was driven out, at which point he directed his efforts to the Gentiles. Paul encountered serious opposition at Ephesus from the silversmiths of the city. Seeing Paul as a threat to their business (which focused largely on making idols), they enacted a riot in which they portrayed Paul as the archenemy of their city and the temple of Artemis. Paul could have been killed had it not been for the intervention of others. In order to remain true to the gospel, Paul witnessed of the only true God by revealing the foolishness of worshiping idols. Likewise, we should stand counter cultural to our communities whenever its values run contrary to the truth of the Scriptures. When we speak out, we may become a disrupting presence and may expect conflict and criticism. Only when we are willing to risk our pride and reputation will we really be able to make a difference in our world.

H

E

A

R

204//1 CORINTHIANS 1–2

MEMORY VERSES: 1 CORINTHIANS 1:18; 1 THESSALONIANS 5:23-24

During Paul's time in Ephesus, he received a troubling report about the state of the church in Corinth, so he wrote a letter to them, which is included in Scripture. One of the main issues facing this church was a lack of unity. Many teachers, some of whom presented different messages, visited the churches in the New Testament. As a result, various factions that favored one Christian leader over another threatened the unity of the church and undermined its effectiveness. Paul's solution was to focus the church's attention solely on Christ and His message, which includes the gift of the Holy Spirit and the wisdom He brings. People without Christ do not have the Holy Spirit to aid them in comprehending God's revealed truth, which is the reason they do not receive what comes from God's Spirit. However, those indwelt with the Spirit of the Lord have the mind of Christ. Although no human being can know everything about God, our understanding of Him and His purposes always has room to expand. God will give us the needed spiritual insight to understand more about Him through the Holy Spirit's involvement in our lives.

H

E

A

R

205//1 CORINTHIANS 3–4

MEMORY VERSES: 1 CORINTHIANS 1:18; 1 THESSALONIANS 5:23-24

The lack of unity in the Corinthian church proved to Paul that these Christians were still infants, or babies, in their spiritual maturity. This is why he focused much of his letter on instructing and reminding them about how to live and mature as followers of Christ in the church. This weakness among them highlighted the importance of the need for spiritual leaders in their church, something they were overlooking. Paul taught that church leaders serve God, and as a result, are accountable first and foremost to Him. Paul insisted that being an effective Christian leader included humbly enduring suffering for the faith, whether physically or through criticism. He sought to present the Corinthians with a servant image of leadership, one that followed Jesus' example. Leadership is a call to serve humbly, not to strut proudly. Above all, they must prove faithful. Paul claimed that all leaders should be evaluated only by the standard of fidelity to Christ, not by eloquence and pretentious human wisdom. When we recognize our accountability to God and pursue His agenda rather than our own, the result will be unity within the church.

H

E

A

R

206//1 CORINTHIANS 5–6

MEMORY VERSES: 1 CORINTHIANS 10:13; 1 CORINTHIANS 13:13

Paul's letters to the Corinthians explain how the believers were in need of spiritual growth and godly leadership. He was stunned by an incident in the church involving a man's misconduct with his stepmother. Apparently, the church ignored this behavior. Paul rebuked both the man and the church. The church was not only to express displeasure with the man's behavior but also to seek to change his behavior. In 6:1-11, Paul further emphasized the responsibility to live morally by addressing the matter of lawsuits between believers. The Corinthian church needed to embrace Christian ethics and reject immoral conduct. Paul closed with a reminder that Christian freedom is not a license to do anything we want but, rather, to embrace Christian morality as God intended. Reflecting on Christ's work of forgiveness and reconciliation in our lives reminds us of our need to repent of sins and rely on His grace.

As you read the Bible this week...

H IGHLIGHT the verses that speak to you.

Write out the name of the book:

Which chapter and verse numbers stand out to you?

E XPLAIN what this passage means.

To whom was it originally written? Why?

How does it fit with the verses before and after it?

What is the Holy Spirit intending to communicate through this text?

A PPLY what God is saying in these verses to your life.

What does this mean today?

What is God saying to you personally?

How can you apply this message to your life?

R ESPOND to what you've read.

In what ways does this passage call you to action?

How will you be different because of what you've learned?

Write out a prayer to God in response to what you read today:

207//1 CORINTHIANS 7–8

MEMORY VERSES: 1 CORINTHIANS 10:13; 1 CORINTHIANS 13:13

Generally speaking, the first six chapters of 1 Corinthians are Paul's response to a report he had received with some alarming revelations about the conduct of some church members in Corinth. After dealing with these matters, Paul shifted to dealing with questions the Corinthians had raised in a letter to him. The Corinthians' first question concerned marriage and sexuality. Having addressed sexual immorality in chapters 5–6, Paul moved to address a related question from their letter. His topics in chapter 7 are abstinence, conduct within a marriage, grateful acceptance of the life to which God calls each person, and potential blessings of singleness. Whether married or single, every Christian should be a slave of Christ. We are to live fully given over to Jesus and the spread of His gospel. One of the great paradoxes in the Christian faith is that only through submission to Christ do we find true freedom. This is a recurring theme in Paul's letters. Living for God is more important than everything else in life.

H

E

A

R

208//1 CORINTHIANS 9–10

MEMORY VERSES: 1 CORINTHIANS 10:13; 1 CORINTHIANS 13:13

The city of Corinth was known for its immorality and perversion, which created a challenging atmosphere for new Christians to live out their faith. To compound the problems, many of the Corinthian Christians were impressed with their own knowledge and spirituality. This pride led to insensitivity in their relationships with other Christians and inappropriate conduct. Paul addressed some of their questions about behavior in chapters 8–9. The first concerned whether Christians should eat food that had been offered to idols. Although Paul agreed with those who asserted that idols are nothing, he reminded them that Christians also need to consider how their actions might impact other believers who don't share their same conviction. Christians show maturity when they avoid behavior that isn't inherently sinful but still might hinder another believer's spiritual growth. In verses 9:1-27, Paul used himself as an example of this principle. He didn't want any of his actions to hinder him in sharing the gospel. Paul regularly emphasized his goal of reaching people for Christ and leading them to a more focused discipleship. For him, that mission trumped every other consideration.

H

E

A

R

209//1 CORINTHIANS 11–12

MEMORY VERSES: 1 CORINTHIANS 10:13; 1 CORINTHIANS 13:13

In 1 Corinthians 10:1–11, Paul returned to the issue of food that had been offered to idols. He did so in the context of helping his readers better understand Christian freedom. As Christians, his readers had an obligation to resist all forms of temptation. Paul urged mature Christians to embrace the responsibility of seeking what was good for other believers over insisting they were free in Christ to engage in certain activities. Paul also addressed the matter of proper conduct in worship. Specific questions concerned head coverings, fellowship meals, and the Lord's Supper. The problems concerning these issues revolved around selfish behavior that was inconsistent with the holy lives they were called to lead. With freedom in Christ comes great responsibility. As new creations in Christ, we need to choose things that further God's kingdom and mission over things that hold us back. This means allowing someone else to rule and lead our lives and require us to abandon our will and control. Following Christ gives us a desire to change our ways and a desire for the gospel to be known.

H

E

A

R

210//1 CORINTHIANS 13–14

MEMORY VERSES: 1 CORINTHIANS 10:13; 1 CORINTHIANS 13:13

Among the many problems the Corinthian church faced, one thorny issue centered on the nature and purpose of spiritual gifts. Some church members viewed the type of gift a believer possessed as a measuring stick for their level of spirituality. In response to this issue, Paul set out a basic rule for consideration of all spiritual gifts—all Christians share the common confession of faith: Jesus is Lord. On this foundation Paul affirmed the value of spiritual gifts and insisted they were not a means for ranking Christians. He listed various gifts and declared that each gift came from one and the same source—the Holy Spirit. Using the analogy of the body, Paul argued that every gift is necessary; therefore, every Christian is important. All gifts, no matter what purpose they serve in the church, must be governed by Christlike love, which he elaborated on in chapter 13. Without Christlike love as their motive, spiritual gifts are empty shells. Love expressed is the way church members then and today are to demonstrate they are the body of Christ on earth. Furthermore, Paul reminded them in chapter 14 that when the church gathers for worship, the purpose should always be to exalt God and strengthen all who are present.

H

E

A

R

211// 1 CORINTHIANS 15–16

MEMORY VERSES: ROMANS 1:16-17; 1 CORINTHIANS 15:3-4

A chief purpose of 1 Corinthians was to answer questions from the church, particularly about the resurrection. Some were questioning the resurrection. They didn't doubt Jesus' resurrection, but they failed to see how it guaranteed that God would raise all believers. The natural connection between Jesus' resurrection and that of believers dovetails out of our union with Christ, a major theme throughout Corinthians. These verses describe human history from the fall of Adam to the consummation of God's kingdom. Every Christ-follower's story ends with resurrection and eternal communion with Christ, which reminds us that we are not to live only for the present day. Because our actions have eternal consequences, each day's choices are important. The future hope of being with Christ and being made new affects every aspect of our Christian life. We live for the greater cause because everything we do for Christ matters eternally.

As you read the Bible this week...

H IGHLIGHT the verses that speak to you.

Write out the name of the book:

Which chapter and verse numbers stand out to you?

E XPLAIN what this passage means.

To whom was it originally written? Why?

How does it fit with the verses before and after it?

What is the Holy Spirit intending to communicate through this text?

A PPLY what God is saying in these verses to your life.

What does this mean today?

What is God saying to you personally?

How can you apply this message to your life?

R ESPOND to what you've read.

In what ways does this passage call you to action?

How will you be different because of what you've learned?

Write out a prayer to God in response to what you read today:

212//2 CORINTHIANS 1–2

MEMORY VERSES: ROMANS 1:16-17; 1 CORINTHIANS 15:3-4

Paul wrote a handful of letters to the church in Corinth, but only two of them made it into Scripture. The purpose of 2 Corinthians is to express Paul's joy in the good report he received about the church, to strengthen his ties with individual church members, to confront outsiders who were trying to undermine Paul's ministry at the church, and to encourage the Corinthian believers to refocus their efforts by participating in a relief offering. In 2 Corinthians 1–2, we witness the vital connection between Paul's commitment to Christ and his commitment to working out difficult relationships. One of the truths about God that we cannot miss is that we serve a God who keeps His promises, something we have seen proven true throughout Scripture. Paul described the promises of God as being "yes" in Christ. We know that God will keep His promises to us because He has proven Himself trustworthy through the life, death, and resurrection of Jesus Christ. He is the same yesterday, today, and for eternity. Because God keeps His promises, we can wait confidently for all of them to be fulfilled. With this confidence in God's promises, we are able to follow in Paul's footsteps of unrelenting commitment to the gospel.

H

E

A

R

213//2 CORINTHIANS 3—4

MEMORY VERSES: ROMANS 1:16-17; 1 CORINTHIANS 15:3-4

Although things were going well in Corinth, Paul did have some opponents there who were raising doubts about his message and motives. Paul responded to these opponents by reminding the Corinthians of his qualifications and his work among them. To prove his case, Paul highlighted all the suffering he had endured, and he contended that his suffering proved that ministry success rested in God's power, not human accomplishments. To help his readers understand, Paul used the imagery of jars of clay, which people in his day owned to hold their most valuable possessions. God has given His people the greatest treasure in the universe—the gospel of Jesus Christ. But believing in this treasure does not make us immune to pain. Instead, we have this treasure in our clay-like lives. Just as people of the time had to shatter the clay jars in which they kept their valuables to reveal the treasure, so God must at times break His people for the gospel to shine forth. When a person is broken, Jesus shines through. God uses these breaking circumstances to bring Himself glory and mold us into His image.

H

E

A

R

214//2 CORINTHIANS 5–6

MEMORY VERSES: ROMANS 1:16-17; 1 CORINTHIANS 15:3-4

Because of the hardships Christians endure living for the gospel, which Paul described in chapter 4, it is important that we learn to set our eyes on eternity. Suffering because of Christ is preparation for eternity because it challenges us to faithfully serve God and live each day for our future with Him. While eternity holds the promise of hope for the Christian, it brings the promise of judgment and condemnation for those who do not know Jesus, which is why Paul also emphasized the importance of the ministry of reconciliation, both with God and with others. Paul's motivation for seeking reconciliation with others was God's love. Christ's love compelled him to continue loving and reaching out to the Corinthians, even when they wronged him. He couldn't accept reconciliation from God and then refuse to pursue reconciliation with other believers. As we recognize the true price for our sin, we should be more and more grateful for Jesus' willing sacrifice on our behalf. As we grow to understand our identity in Christ, we will embrace the great task with which God has blessed us in Christ—to be His "ambassadors" of Christ's message of reconciliation.

H

E

A

R

215//2 CORINTHIANS 7—8

MEMORY VERSES: ROMANS 1:16-17; 1 CORINTHIANS 15:3-4

Second Corinthians 7 provides additional insight into Paul's interaction with the church at Corinth. He had received a report from Titus concerning the church and rejoiced that their once-strained relationship was improving. Paul's goal throughout his long-distance relationship with Corinth was to maintain love and intimacy. Moving to more practical matters, Paul addressed the need for a relief offering for needy Christians in Jerusalem. Sacrificial generosity was a practice the church established at its conception in Acts 2; therefore, Paul reminds the church that generosity should be fundamental in their ministry to one another. He told the Corinthians about the generosity of the Macedonian churches who—despite their own poverty—had raised money for the poor Christians in Jerusalem. Even though they were poor, they gave generously because the Christian community was in need. Second Corinthians 8:9 reveals what should motivate all believers to willingly sacrifice of themselves for the sake of others—Jesus' sacrifice for us. Jesus practiced and taught sacrificial giving. Gratitude for what Jesus has done for us motivates us to demonstrate responsible stewardship of our lives and our possessions.

H

E

A

R

216//2 CORINTHIANS 9–10

MEMORY VERSES: 2 CORINTHIANS 10:4; ROMANS 5:1

Continuing the topic of giving, Paul challenged the Corinthians to give freely and cheerfully, not by compulsion, so their gift would be a blessing—not only to the recipients but to the givers as well. The same attitude should characterize our acts of giving today. After reminding the Corinthians that giving in this matter would be a witness to others, Paul switched his topic and tone. Paul aimed to confront "certain people" in the church who were undermining him and his coworkers. He belonged to God, and his motives for serving God were pure. Defending himself and his teaching, Paul reminds his readers then and now that we are in a spiritual battle (10:2-5). We must guard against any thinking that can interfere with our growth in Christ and our witness for Him. By calling us to take our thoughts captive, Paul reminds us that we must align our thoughts with the things of Christ.

As you read the Bible this week...

H IGHLIGHT the verses that speak to you.

Write out the name of the book:

Which chapter and verse numbers stand out to you?

E XPLAIN what this passage means.

To whom was it originally written? Why?

How does it fit with the verses before and after it?

What is the Holy Spirit intending to communicate through this text?

A PPLY what God is saying in these verses to your life.

What does this mean today?

What is God saying to you personally?

How can you apply this message to your life?

R ESPOND to what you've read.

In what ways does this passage call you to action?

How will you be different because of what you've learned?

Write out a prayer to God in response to what you read today:

217//2 CORINTHIANS 11–13

MEMORY VERSES: 2 CORINTHIANS 10:4; ROMANS 5:1

In the closing section of his letter, Paul conveyed his concerns about the Corinthians. Though reluctant to appear harsh, Paul refused to allow his critics to mischaracterize and undermine his Christian service. Rather than call attention to his knowledge, experience, and abilities, Paul cited all of his struggles as evidence of his integrity and devotion to Christ. Through all of these difficulties, which included a thorn in his flesh that God would not remove, Paul learned the life-changing truth that God's power is demonstrated in the midst of human weakness. Rather than removing Paul's suffering, God gave him something better—sufficient grace for Paul to rise above it by depending on God's power. Like Paul, our own weaknesses open the door for God's power to flow through us, changing not only our lives but also the lives of those we come in contact with. Paul closed his second letter to the Corinthians with the promise to visit them again, which further challenged them to pursue spiritual growth and maturity in Christ.

H _____

E _____

_____

_____

A _____

_____

_____

R _____

_____

_____

218//ROMANS 1–2; ACTS 20:1-3

MEMORY VERSES: 2 CORINTHIANS 10:4; ROMANS 5:1

During Paul's third missionary journey, he spent time in Greece, at which time he wrote his letter to the Romans. Paul's plan was to make his way to Rome, so he wrote this letter to the Christians there in order to communicate his life calling and the message he longed to tell others. Paul was writing to proclaim the gospel, a message built on the foundation of the Old Testament and fulfilled in Jesus Christ. To establish the universal need for the gospel, Paul pointed to the undeniable presence of sin in our world and our lives. At its core, sin is idolatry: the worship of the creation instead of the Creator. Paul declared that God will render His judgment on those whose hearts are unrepentant. But He will give eternal life to those who show by their actions that they have His Law written on their hearts. Paul's main point is this: Until we realize we are sinners by nature, we won't realize our desperate need for salvation and appreciate God's grace.

H

E

A

R

219//ROMANS 3–4

MEMORY VERSES: 2 CORINTHIANS 10:4; ROMANS 5:1

Paul spent a good portion of Romans helping the Jews understand how they needed God's grace as much as Gentiles (non-Jews) do. The truth that all people stand condemned for sin means that Jews and Gentiles are equally guilty before God. No one can be justified by the works of the Law, which is why everyone needs Jesus. Only by grace through faith in Him can a person experience salvation. Paul reminded his Jewish readers that the covenant promises God made to Abraham and his descendants were assured by faith, not by the Law. God's promises were a display of grace to Abraham and to all who respond to God with faith like Abraham's, faith that trusts God to give life to the dead and to call things into existence that do not exist. For Paul, such an example as Abraham's was proof that the gospel of Jesus Christ both continued and fulfilled what had always been God's plan of salvation. Those who come to God by placing their faith in Jesus will find they are forgiven of sins and have been made right with God.

H

E

A

R

220//ROMANS 5–6

MEMORY VERSES: 2 CORINTHIANS 10:4; ROMANS 5:1

Paul began Romans 5 by focusing on the present benefits of peace, hope, and love from God, all benefits that a believer can count on every day. God doesn't save us by grace only to make us then try to live for Him in our own power. God's grace is given to help us stand today, tomorrow, and on that future day when we will stand before His throne. Paul also described how God redeemed us when we were at our worst, which demonstrates just how great His grace is. In Romans 6, Paul discussed reasons that Christians can no longer think and live in the old ways of sin. Believers have died to the old life by being baptized into Jesus' death and raised into new life through His resurrection. We serve a new Master who freed us from bondage to sin and empowers us to grow in faith, thus producing the spiritual fruit that shows we have eternal life. Through our obedience, we display Christ and His character to the world. Only by allowing Christ to live in us can we truly have an impact for the kingdom of God.

H

E

A

R

221//ROMANS 7–8

MEMORY VERSES: ROMANS 8:1; ROMANS 12:1-2

Paul used marriage as an illustration of being dead to sin and free from the Law's condemning power. Christians can serve God freely by His Spirit. Still, the Law makes us aware of our sinfulness and guides us to Christ. Paul concluded by focusing on the power and presence of Jesus Christ in his life in contrast to his own struggle with sin. Through Christ, the Spirit's power enables us to live in ways that honor God. The Spirit helps us resist sin and provides guidance in making decisions. Furthermore, the Spirit confirms that we are God's children. We are adopted into God's family and can go to God as Father. Because of this, nothing we face can be compared to the glory that awaits us. Our hope in Christ is certain. Though we often feel discouraged, we have a limitless source of hope. Our challenge is to patiently persevere in the face of any present difficulty. Paul closed Romans 8 by affirming God is at work in all things.

As you read the Bible this week...

H I G H L I G H T the verses that speak to you.

Write out the name of the book:

Which chapter and verse numbers stand out to you?

E X P L A I N what this passage means.

To whom was it originally written? Why?

How does it fit with the verses before and after it?

What is the Holy Spirit intending to communicate through this text?

A P P L Y what God is saying in these verses to your life.

What does this mean today?

What is God saying to you personally?

How can you apply this message to your life?

R E S P O N D to what you've read.

In what ways does this passage call you to action?

How will you be different because of what you've learned?

Write out a prayer to God in response to what you read today:

222//ROMANS 9–10

MEMORY VERSES: ROMANS 8:1; ROMANS 12:1-2

In Romans 1–8, Paul developed the doctrine of salvation by faith alone. He concluded that God's purposes for His people can never fail. However, it seemed that His purposes for the Israelite people had indeed failed because most of them rejected Jesus as their Messiah. Paul addressed this issue in chapter 9. He emphasized that God is sovereign in all things, including matters of salvation. Next, he explained that God was not being unjust toward those He did not choose by focusing on God's mercy, something that is utterly undeserved and can never be earned. Paul used Pharaoh to illustrate his point of one who did not receive God's mercy. Then Paul emphasized God's patience to Jews and Gentiles alike. The result is that members of both races have access to His mercy and to be saved. For the most part, the Israelites had tried to obtain salvation by obeying God's Law, but no humans can ever save themselves regardless of how zealous they are. No one can do enough good works to earn or receive salvation. Faith—simply believing—and the grace that comes by it is the only way to a right relationship with God.

H

E

A

R

223//ROMANS 11–12

MEMORY VERSES: ROMANS 8:1; ROMANS 12:1-2

God has a great plan for history that includes saving many people—both Jews and Gentiles. At the time when Paul wrote, God's saving purposes centered on many Gentiles coming to faith in God. The day will come when God's saving plan will be accomplished as Jews and Gentiles acknowledge Him as both Lord and Savior. Our response should be praise for the wonder of His saving plan. Chapter 12 marks the most important transition in Romans as Paul moves to the "So what?" question. What difference should salvation make in the life of a believer? The first effect of salvation is that we offer ourselves to God in sacrifice and worship by committing to live for Him. We are to seek transformation in how we think through the Word of God, which will result in knowing and experiencing the will of God as well as worshiping God. Our salvation impacts the church body too as we use our spiritual gifts wisely to serve others. Paul was aware that it is possible to exercise the gifts of the Spirit without displaying the fruit of the Spirit—specifically, love. For that reason, he took some time to remind his readers that Christian love is genuine, opposed to evil, and committed to what is good.

H

E

A

R

224//ROMANS 13–14

In Romans 12, Paul dealt with how a follower of Christ is to relate to God and to the church. As he continues to unpack the effects of salvation in a person's life, he provides instruction on how salvation impacts a person's relationship with government and neighbors, whether Christian or not. As far as government is concerned, Christians are expected to show respect for leaders and to pay taxes. Paul reminded his readers that the Ten Commandments teach us how to love one's neighbors. Jesus' disciples are also expected to maintain high moral standards in daily relationships—specifically, in sexual behavior, sobriety, and integrity of speech. Paul's words in Romans 14 continue the theme of relationships with others by encouraging us to maintain unity by not judging others for their convictions and not causing others to stumble into sin. God's kingdom is more important than our rights, so we need to let love determine how we act toward one another.

H

E

A

R

225//ROMANS 15–16

MEMORY VERSES: ROMANS 8:1; ROMANS 12:1-2

Paul closes his letter to the Romans by calling to mind two examples that help us understand the actions and attitudes our salvation should bring forth—the examples of Jesus and of Paul himself. We glorify God by living in harmony with one another and by remembering the life of the Lord Jesus. Christians ought to treat others the same way Jesus treats His people—with compassion, sacrifice, and grace. Paul also voiced his desire for the Romans to be filled with abundant hope through the Holy Spirit. Paul concluded this letter with personal information about his plans to spread the gospel even farther. As he brought his letter to a close, Paul issued a short warning against those who would disrupt the unity of the church, then complimented the Romans once more for their reputation. Fittingly, the final words of his letter are praise to God for His greatness and glory.

H

E

A

R

226//ACTS 20–21

MEMORY VERSES: ACTS 20:24; 2 CORINTHIANS 4:7-10

Paul was finishing up his third period of missionary activity. Having spent three years in Ephesus, he departed, evidently shortly after the episode with the silversmiths. Paul traveled through Macedonia, revisiting the churches there, then went on to Corinth in Greece. Acts 20-21 record several stops on this missionary journey. Among the notable things in these chapters are Paul's words of encouragement to the leaders of the church at Ephesus and the repeated warnings he received about the dangers that awaited him at Jerusalem because of his faith. Despite several warnings, Paul continued on to Jerusalem. At the temple, Paul was attacked by a mob. He likely would have been killed had the Romans not taken him into custody. These two chapters reveal Paul's undivided focus on spreading the gospel. When we are fully convinced of who Jesus is and what He has done, we will be obedient to His call and passionate about His priorities.

As you read the Bible this week...

HIGHLIGHT the verses that speak to you.

Write out the name of the book:

Which chapter and verse numbers stand out to you?

EXPLAIN what this passage means.

To whom was it originally written? Why?

How does it fit with the verses before and after it?

What is the Holy Spirit intending to communicate through this text?

APPLY what God is saying in these verses to your life.

What does this mean today?

What is God saying to you personally?

How can you apply this message to your life?

RESPOND to what you've read.

In what ways does this passage call you to action?

How will you be different because of what you've learned?

Write out a prayer to God in response to what you read today:

227//ACTS 22–23

MEMORY VERSES: ACTS 20:24; 2 CORINTHIANS 4:7-10

Chapters 22–23 relate the events surrounding Paul's imprisonment in Jerusalem and his transfer to Caesarea. After he was arrested, Paul addressed the Jewish mob in the temple courtyard—the same mob that moments before sought to kill him. Paul's speech included proof of his Roman citizenship and of his Jewish identity, as well as a description of Jesus' call in Paul's life—a call he was being obedient to follow, even in chains. When the angry crowd abruptly ended Paul's speech, he was taken into the Roman barracks. A Roman centurion was ordered to flog and interrogate Paul to determine the true nature of the Jews' grievances against him. Paul revealed his Roman citizenship to the centurion, who quickly informed his commanding officer. From that point on, the Romans treated Paul much differently. This situation grieved Paul deeply. In the midst of such circumstances, God reminded Paul that He is always at work and that He would empower Paul to preach the gospel in Rome. God's Word and God's work in our lives strengthens us to continue living for Him.

H

E

A

R

228//ACTS 24–25

MEMORY VERSES: ACTS 20:24; 2 CORINTHIANS 4:7-10

The governor Felix called for a hearing of Paul's case. Although Paul's accusers brought serious charges against him, they were unable to prove his guilt, leading Felix to postpone the trial. (Felix never reconvened Paul's trial.) He kept Paul under confinement throughout the remaining two years of his term as governor. Once Felix's replacement came along, the Jewish leaders requested Paul be brought to Jerusalem for trial. Realizing the danger to his life of traveling to Jerusalem, Paul exercised his right as a Roman citizen to appeal to Caesar. Festus accepted the appeal, thus setting Paul's course for Rome. Festus, too, had a hard time knowing how to handle Paul's case, since he could find no clear source of guilt. Not long after Paul made his appeal to Caesar (25:12), the Jewish king Agrippa arrived in Caesarea. Festus hoped Agrippa would counsel him in what to do. Throughout his ministry, Paul seized every opportunity to share the gospel with others, and God continually opened doors to make that a reality. Similarly, when we truly grasp the love God demonstrated for us through the death and resurrection of His Son, it compels us to live for Him and to share that joy with others.

H

E

A

R

229//ACTS 26–27

MEMORY VERSES: ACTS 20:24; 2 CORINTHIANS 4:7-10

Because King Agrippa voiced interest in hearing from Paul, the apostle had the opportunity to defend himself and his gospel ministry before the king. Paul's testimony became the basis for an appeal. He pressed the king to acknowledge Christ as the Savior foretold by the prophets. The king rose to his feet and ended the hearing. As he departed with Festus, the two agreed on Paul's innocence. Paul was then sent to Rome to appear before Caesar. The journey to Rome ordinarily took a couple of months at most, but Paul's party encountered bad weather, delaying the trip six more months. Because of the weather, the ship sailed off course from its normal route. When the crew failed to heed Paul's advice, disaster resulted in the form of a massive storm. In the midst of the crew and passengers' despair, Paul predicted that they all would be delivered, which happened just as he said. Paul's life proves time and again that when we are faithful to God's direction, He remains by our side and sees us through. God gives us innumerable promises to help us endure our storms and point others to Christ.

H

E

A

R

230//ACTS 28

The ship on which Paul was traveling wrecked on the island of Malta, which is south of Sicily. Paul immediately impressed the island's inhabitants when God delivered him unharmed from a viper's bite. This allowed him to carry out a ministry of healing among them. After the winter had passed and the seas were again safe for travel, Paul's party secured passage to Italy. As they completed their journey to Rome on foot, Paul was met by two separate groups of Roman Christians who had come out to greet him. Once in the city, Paul was allowed to live in an apartment rented at his own expense so long as he remained imprisoned under military guard. Luke's story ends with Paul being under house arrest in Rome for two years as he awaited his hearing before Caesar. During that time, he freely witnessed to all who came to hear him share the gospel. Paul could have easily allowed his circumstances to override his proclamation of the gospel, but instead of throwing in the towel, he continued to proclaim God's love. We should do the same. Christ calls us to make the most of every opportunity to share the gospel with others.

H

E

A

R

231//COLOSSIANS 1–2

MEMORY VERSES: EPHESIANS 2:8-10; COLOSSIANS 2:6-7

Paul wrote to the Colossians during his first imprisonment in Rome. The letter corrected misunderstandings by false teachers urging believers to blend other religious ideas with Christianity. The theme is the centrality of Christ. Though Paul did not know many of the believers personally, he was concerned for their spiritual welfare. He affirmed Christ's deity as well as His lordship over creation. Paul maintained that Jesus is the Creator and Sustainer of all things. He is more than able to reconcile us to God through His cross. Next, Paul attacked a false teaching that had become a problem for Christians in Colossae. He challenged believers to continue their commitment and gratitude to Christ. Our lives should be grounded on the foundation of Jesus, and our faith should be fixed on Him as a result. When we see Jesus like this and lose sight of our own lives in His greatness, we understand who we truly are and for what we were created.

As you read the Bible this week...

H IGHLIGHT the verses that speak to you.

Write out the name of the book:

Which chapter and verse numbers stand out to you?

E XPLAIN what this passage means.

To whom was it originally written? Why?

How does it fit with the verses before and after it?

What is the Holy Spirit intending to communicate through this text?

A PPLY what God is saying in these verses to your life.

What does this mean today?

What is God saying to you personally?

How can you apply this message to your life?

R ESPOND to what you've read.

In what ways does this passage call you to action?

How will you be different because of what you've learned?

Write out a prayer to God in response to what you read today:

232//COLOSSIANS 3–4

Colossians 1–2 form the doctrinal section of Colossians, while chapters 3–4 compose the practical part of Paul's letter. After the apostle had dealt with theological issues facing the Colossians, he proceeded to turn to practical concerns related to their daily lives and their call to pursue holy living. Paul reminded them that, through their conversion experiences, the Colossian believers had died to their old way of life and had risen with Christ to walk in newness of life, as symbolized through baptism. With that reminder, Paul then dealt with some of the most prevalent sins of the first-century Greco-Roman world. He provided a list of attitudes and behaviors the Colossians were to "put to death" (3:5). In contrast, Paul also provided a list of virtues these believers were to "put on" (3:12). If the Colossians were to genuinely serve Christ, they had to conduct their lives in a manner worthy of Him. Even today, such qualities should be evident in our lives as a result of a right relationship with Christ. We have been given the responsibility to reflect Christ to the world, which means we are to pursue His holiness in all we say and do.

H

E

A

R

233//EPHESIANS 1–2

Paul's purpose with the letter to the Ephesians was to communicate God's redemptive plan and power and then to challenge his readers to become everything God wanted them to be as His people. Paul describes at length the wonder of God's plan of salvation. Paul revealed that God's plan is much more extensive than simply saving individual people in isolation. God gives of His power to the church to enable believers to live for Him and to carry out His gospel mission in the world. Paul also reminded his readers of how desperate and depraved their condition was before they responded to the gospel. He then declared the power of God's undeserved grace toward them. Finally, he summarized the way in which believers' good works are the result of salvation. Paul then emphasized the relational dimension of salvation. What matters most about us is not what the world tells us, how people see us, or even how we see ourselves. Our identity is determined by what God says about us. Apart from Christ, we were dead and hopeless. But in Christ, we are alive and will live forever with Him. When we begin believing what God says about us, we can find the freedom to walk in the good works He has planned for us.

H

E

A

R

234//EPHESIANS 3–4

MEMORY VERSES: EPHESIANS 2:8-10; COLOSSIANS 2:6-7

In Ephesians 2, Paul had developed his understanding of God's salvation. Here in Ephesians 3, Paul pointedly reminded readers of his personal role in spreading the good news. Paul's ministry was a gift of grace—an example of accepting opportunities to serve God. As Paul wrapped up this part of the letter, he was compelled to pray for his readers yet again. This prayer highlights God's power, Christ's love, and believers' experience of God's power. As we experience God's strength, we will be equipped to fulfill everything to which God calls His people. That is the theme Paul focused on in the second half of his epistle. Right thinking about God and salvation will have a practical effect on the way a believer lives today. After reminding them that God had called them to "walk worthy," Paul reviewed the matter of spiritual gifts. He then urged believers to work together for their collective good, using the analogy of a physical body growing to maturity. Paul also contrasted the behavior of Christians with the behavior of non-Christians. Simply put, believers are to live differently. We are to be different in our moral behavior, our desires, our speech, our relationships, our priorities, and our very identities.

H

E

A

R

235//EPHESIANS 5–6

MEMORY VERSES: EPHESIANS 2:8-10; COLOSSIANS 2:6-7

In Ephesians 4, Paul described how Christians are to live uniquely and distinctly, set apart for Christ. Because God is love, we are to extend His love toward others. Because God is pure in speech and behavior, we are to behave without impurity. Because God is light, we are to live as children of the light. As Paul continued writing to the Ephesian Christians about how God expects His people to behave, he came to consider family relationships. After all, if one's faith does not measurably make marriages stronger, or make for a better relationship between parents and children, it will be difficult to commend others to do the same. A married person's relationship with Christ should form the foundation of an enduring and joyous relationship with their spouse. Paul went on to consider the impact that knowing the Lord Jesus has on other relationships. Those relationships include the parent-child relationship and the employer-employee relationship. Paul closed with a call to be prepared for the spiritual battle the Christian life inevitably demands. We live prepared by putting on the armor of God, always available to His children. No matter what we face, we must rely on the immovable strength and protection of God.

H

E

A

R

236//PHILIPPIANS 1–2

MEMORY VERSES: PHILIPPIANS 3:7-8; HEBREWS 4:14-16

Paul's letter to the Philippians was deeply personal. They had helped him in the past, and during his imprisonment they again came to his aid. Paul assured them of his thankfulness for their partnership. He prayed their love would continue to grow as they discerned the most important things in life and thus prepared to face God's judgment with confidence. Paul viewed his circumstances as a part of God's greater plan for the spread of the gospel, but these verses also reflect the tension he felt within himself. Paul was not afraid of death, but he felt torn between the desire to be with Christ and the desire to remain in the flesh and help the Philippians grow in the faith. Whatever the outcome, Paul had the assurance that Christ would be glorified. As Paul encouraged his friends, he cited the example of Christ to inspire unity and humility. When we imitate Christ, we shine as His light in the world, displaying the good news of the gospel.

As you read the Bible this week...

H I G H L I G H T the verses that speak to you.

Write out the name of the book:

Which chapter and verse numbers stand out to you?

E X P L A I N what this passage means.

To whom was it originally written? Why?

How does it fit with the verses before and after it?

What is the Holy Spirit intending to communicate through this text?

A P P L Y what God is saying in these verses to your life.

What does this mean today?

What is God saying to you personally?

How can you apply this message to your life?

R E S P O N D to what you've read.

In what ways does this passage call you to action?

How will you be different because of what you've learned?

Write out a prayer to God in response to what you read today:

237//PHILIPPIANS 3—4

MEMORY VERSES: PHILIPPIANS 3:7-8; HEBREWS 4:14-16

The third chapter of Philippians deals with Paul's personal experience in Christ. He referred to his background in Judaism and contrasted it with his present life in Christ. Though Paul experienced every privilege Judaism offered, he did not regret his decision to follow Christ. In fact, he considered his past to be rubbish compared to Christ. Paul described his life in Christ as one of continual striving to reach the goal of maturity in Christ. Further, he exhorted the Philippians to imitate him in their quest for spiritual maturity. In chapter 4 of Philippians, Paul concluded his message to his friends by challenging, instructing, and thanking them. Though the Philippians had struggles, Paul still loved them and encouraged them to grow in their relationship with Christ and to focus on eternity at all times. Our relationship with Christ involves a growing and personal understanding with Him, which shapes our entire outlook on life. We become spiritually stagnant when we allow our good works to manipulate us into thinking we are not in need of spiritual growth. We also become spiritually sidetracked when we allow past failures to stifle future maturity.

H

E

A

R

238//HEBREWS 1–2

Although the writer of the Book of Hebrews is unknown, its purpose is clear: Hebrews was written to content Christians who needed encouragement to grow into mature followers of Christ. Throughout Hebrews, the writer emphasized Jesus' superiority to everything the Jews' religious system offered. The writer began by declaring that, in the past, God had spoken through the prophets, but now, God spoke through His Son Jesus. The writer went on to list five descriptions of Jesus that stressed His deity, redemptive death, and exaltation. The writer warned believers against neglecting the salvation God provided through His Son. He next presented the argument for why God's Son became human. God gave humans the assignment of managing His creation. People, however, had not done so. Genesis 3 makes clear that sin had prevented people from fulfilling God's purpose for them. Hebrews 2 shows that Jesus became human to provide a solution to mankind's sin problem. He did for people what they could not do for themselves. Through His death, He made salvation available. In this way, Jesus is the High Priest who gave Himself for people so they could be forgiven. Only through faith in God can people reach the fulfillment of all that He made them to be.

H

E

A

R

239//HEBREWS 3—4

MEMORY VERSES: PHILIPPIANS 3:7-8; HEBREWS 4:14-16

In chapter 3, the writer turned to the examples or models of faithfulness that both Jesus and Moses gave. While Moses was a faithful servant among God's people, Jesus is the faithful Son over God's people. Then the writer quoted Psalm 95:7-11 as a warning against the readers being unfaithful to God and rebelling against Him. They were to be careful not to harden their hearts against God's will. Furthermore, they were not to allow unbelief to cause them to stand off from God and His will for them. Rather, they were to encourage one another daily and to be true to their professions of faith in Christ. In chapter 4, the writer expressed his desire that his readers obey God and enter His rest—the spiritual reality of which the promised land was a symbol. The writer stressed that genuine believers have entered God's rest through faith and obedience. Because God sees us as we are, we must confess and repent of our sins so we can be forgiven. Then we will find true, unshakable rest that transcends the circumstances of life.

H

E

A

R

240//HEBREWS 5–6

Just as God called the Israelites' high priests to their roles, He also called Jesus to be the ultimate High Priest. Unlike human high priests, however, Jesus was sinless—He did not need to offer sacrifices for Himself. Jesus is qualified, as God's Son who died for people's sins, to be Savior and High Priest for everyone who will trust Him. The writer then turned to the problem of his readers' spiritual immaturity. He lamented over the fact that his readers should have been spiritually mature but were not. They needed someone to teach them the basic Christian doctrines. They were still spiritual infants, so his advice was to take deliberate action to grow in their faith, love, and hope. They were not to become lazy but were to imitate worthy examples of faith and perseverance. At the close of chapter 6, we are reminded that God's faithfulness to His promises should encourage believers to maintain their hope in Him and in eternity. Because of Jesus' high priesthood, we have solid hope anchored in what Jesus has done on our behalf.

H _____

_____

E _____

_____

_____

_____

A _____

_____

_____

R _____

_____

_____

_____

241//HEBREWS 7

MEMORY VERSES: GALATIANS 2:19-20; 2 CORINTHIANS 5:17

The writer of Hebrews wrapped up chapter 6 by stating that because of Jesus' high priesthood, believers have hope anchored in what Jesus has done on our behalf. In chapter 7, the writer explains how the priesthood of Melchizedek was far superior to Abraham and Aaron's priesthood. The argument made is that if the sacrificial system under Aaron's priestly line could have redeemed people, no need would have existed for a high priest in Melchizedek's order to come. But it couldn't, so Jesus came as High Priest in that order. Jesus is the Son of God and eternal with God Himself, so the hope provided through Jesus' work as High Priest is guaranteed. Because His priesthood is forever, what Jesus did for the salvation of sinners is permanent, and believers' hope is secure.

As you read the Bible this week...

HIGHLIGHT the verses that speak to you.

Write out the name of the book:

Which chapter and verse numbers stand out to you?

EXPLAIN what this passage means.

To whom was it originally written? Why?

How does it fit with the verses before and after it?

What is the Holy Spirit intending to communicate through this text?

APPLY what God is saying in these verses to your life.

What does this mean today?

What is God saying to you personally?

How can you apply this message to your life?

RESPOND to what you've read.

In what ways does this passage call you to action?

How will you be different because of what you've learned?

Write out a prayer to God in response to what you read today:

242//HEBREWS 8–9

MEMORY VERSES: GALATIANS 2:19-20; 2 CORINTHIANS 5:17

In Hebrews 8–9, the writer continued his emphasis on Jesus as the kind of High Priest believers need by bringing attention to God's Old Testament covenant and the tabernacle under Moses. The writer described Jesus as Priest of the true tabernacle and Mediator of a better covenant. From God's original design, the tabernacle and its rituals were symbols that pointed forward to Jesus and the redemption from sins His sacrifice would bring. He offered the perfect, once-and-for-all sacrifice—Himself. This superior sacrifice can cleanse us and make us fit to serve God. To ratify the old covenant, Moses sprinkled the blood of sacrifices on "the tabernacle and all the articles of worship" (9:21). To ratify the new covenant, Jesus offered His very blood. With His death, Jesus offers us permanent forgiveness for sins and eternal life in the presence of God.

H

E

A

R

243//HEBREWS 10

MEMORY VERSES: GALATIANS 2:19-20; 2 CORINTHIANS 5:17

The writer of Hebrews was convinced that the Jews' sacrificial system was powerless to cleanse people of their sins. He emphasized the system's inability to make anyone right with God and spiritually mature. The repeated sacrifices only reminded the Jews of their sins, that they could not take them away. The writer turned to the Old Testament to show that Jesus accomplished what the old covenant's sacrificial system could not. Through Jesus' perfect sacrifice, people of faith are made right with God and are set on a path to spiritual maturity. In verse 19, the author moves from theological to practical teaching as he gives direction on how people live out their faith in Jesus. Our faith that Jesus is the sinless, eternal High Priest who offered Himself as the perfect, once-for-all sacrifice for ours sins should be reflected in our behavior. The writer urged them to draw near to God in faith and purity, holding firmly to their confession of hope with the assurance of God's faithfulness. They were challenged to encourage one another to love and to do good works while meeting together consistently. He warned them against the danger of sin and the threat of persecution. The instructions in Hebrews 10 remind us that the pursuit of God and the acceptance of sin cannot coexist in the life of the Christian.

H

E

A

R

244//HEBREWS 11

MEMORY VERSES: GALATIANS 2:19-20; 2 CORINTHIANS 5:17

Often referred to as the "Hall of Faith," Hebrews 11 outlines men and women who displayed exceptional faith in God. First, he defines faith in terms of trusting God to the extent of having assurance of His promised blessings. A person cannot please God without faith, so the writer pointed to Noah and Abraham as examples of men who demonstrated faith by their actions. A major aspect of faith is to trust God when we do not experience the fulfillment of all His promises, as Abraham and Sarah modeled. Sometimes we will experience tests of our faith, like Abraham and Moses. Numerous other Old Testament saints demonstrated faith in God. They did not see God's ultimate promise fulfilled, but through their faith God bore witness to its fulfillment. All of these examples show us that genuine faith is demonstrated in our obedience to what God says. Real faith is trusting God with our lives, including our future. God is looking for this kind of faith in His people.

H
_____

E
_____

_____

A
_____

_____

R
_____

_____

245//HEBREWS 12

MEMORY VERSES: GALATIANS 2:19-20; 2 CORINTHIANS 5:17

In Hebrews 11, the writer described what faith looks like for the Christ follower as modeled by the Old Testament saints. In chapter 12, he likened the life of faith as a marathon that requires great endurance. Along the way we will face difficulties, some of which are discipline from God. We can endure these seasons by growing spiritually through such opportunities. Like an earthly father's discipline, which may be painful but yields positive results, God's chastisement of His children is difficult to receive. However, it's always meant for redemption, not condemnation. From this chapter we are also challenged to strive for spiritual health and holiness, and we are encouraged to greater service. When we truly understand the sacrifices God has made to draw us back to Himself, as the writer described earlier in his letter, then we will desire to show Him gratitude, which we do primarily through serving and worshiping Him. Through Christ, we are also united to one another in deeper community.

H

E

A

R

246//1 TIMOTHY 1–3

MEMORY VERSES: 2 TIMOTHY 2:1-2; 2 TIMOTHY 2:15

In addition to the letters Paul wrote to churches, he also wrote letters to individuals whom he discipled to be leaders and pastors. Paul began investing in Timothy's life when he was a teenager. Timothy became a son in the faith to Paul as he accompanied Paul on his missionary journeys. Paul displays humility by reminding him of his own sinfulness and need for Christ's forgiveness. He warns Timothy about false teachers and instructs him on the importance of sound Christian doctrine to combat their heresies. Next, Paul gave Timothy specific instructions about church and worship practices, including prayer, teaching, gender roles, and leadership. All of these reminders prove that our character and actions are important to God, which result in true worship.

As you read the Bible this week...

H I G H L I G H T the verses that speak to you.

Write out the name of the book:

Which chapter and verse numbers stand out to you?

E X P L A I N what this passage means.

To whom was it originally written? Why?

How does it fit with the verses before and after it?

What is the Holy Spirit intending to communicate through this text?

A P P L Y what God is saying in these verses to your life.

What does this mean today?

What is God saying to you personally?

How can you apply this message to your life?

R E S P O N D to what you've read.

In what ways does this passage call you to action?

How will you be different because of what you've learned?

Write out a prayer to God in response to what you read today:

247//1 TIMOTHY 4–6

MEMORY VERSES: 2 TIMOTHY 2:1-2; 2 TIMOTHY 2:15

Paul reminded Timothy that he had been put in a position of responsibility to be a good example to other believers. Paul challenged him by offering a series of reminders about what it means to be a Christian role model. An exemplary Christian should extend respect to those in different life stages, compassion to those who need it, and support to leaders of the church. In chapter 6, Paul emphasizes the foolishness of greed and the wise pursuit of godliness. To make this point, Paul contrasted the eternal benefit of godliness and contentment versus the temporal benefit of material wealth. The love of money is a terrible trap, but those whom God has blessed with riches are expected to use it for the good of God's kingdom. These three chapters emphasize the importance of godly living. The pursuit of godliness is an important aspect of the Christian life, and it's how we ensure we're following God and growing in our faith. When we're devoted to our relationship with God and invested in spiritual training, He uses us to make a difference in the world, just as He used Timothy and Paul.

H

E

A

R

248//2 TIMOTHY 1–2

MEMORY VERSES: 2 TIMOTHY 2:1-2; 2 TIMOTHY 2:15

It is unknown exactly how much time passed between Paul's first letter to Timothy and the second one, but it is clear that Paul's circumstances had changed drastically. The Letter of 2 Timothy is thought to be Paul's last letter, and he wrote it from a prison cell in Rome just prior to his execution. The apostle's sense of urgency is evident throughout this letter. Paul reminded Timothy of the content of the gospel message, which is built upon Jesus. Using himself as the model, Paul reminds Timothy that discipleship should be paramount in his ministry. Effectiveness in ministry would be determined by how well he has passed on what he heard from Paul. He used several illustrations from those who endure hardship in order to achieve a worthwhile goal: soldiers, athletes, and farmers. The various teachings Paul gave in these two chapters were meant to spur Timothy on toward holy living. Paul's teaching to Timothy helps us see that God calls us to regularly practice repentance both by turning away from sin and actively submitting our lives to Christ.

H

E

A

R

249//2 TIMOTHY 3–4

MEMORY VERSES: 2 TIMOTHY 2:1-2; 2 TIMOTHY 2:15

In the second half of 2 Timothy, Paul shifted his focus to the days that lay ahead for Christians, days of persecution and godlessness. Paul identified a number of sinful behaviors that will characterize unbelievers in "the last days." Timothy was to avoid these behaviors and the people practicing them. Instead, Timothy's responsibility was to emphasize God's truth. Paul also warned Timothy to be prepared for persecution and equipped for right living. Timothy's guide—and our guide today—through all these difficulties must be the inspired Word of God, which would profit him in all areas of belief and behavior. Because of the power of God's Word and the prevalence of sin in society, Paul reminded Timothy to preach the Word at all times and in all seasons. To "preach" includes more than standing behind a pulpit to deliver a sermon. We all have opportunities to make known the truth of God's Word. We must live the faith and be available as witnesses to the truth all the time.

H

E

A

R

250//1 PETER 1–2

MEMORY VERSES: 2 TIMOTHY 2:1-2; 2 TIMOTHY 2:15

Included among the books of the New Testament are two letters the apostle Peter wrote to groups of Christians. In his first letter, Peter addressed both Jewish and Gentile Christians who were experiencing violent persecution. Peter wrote to encourage his readers to persevere in their faith and to brace for future attacks. These teachings have implications on our lives as Christ-followers today. The basis for Christian hope is Jesus' resurrection and the promise of eternal life. In light of eternity, our trials are temporary and serve to refine our faith. As we await Jesus' return, we are to live holy lives. In obedience to God, we are to seek to reflect His holiness in our behavior, which is possible because we have been redeemed from our old, sinful way of life. In chapter 2, Peter uses several images to help us understand how we have been changed by Christ. We have been given a new diet ("spiritual milk" that helps us grow in Christlikeness), a new house (the church), and a new family (God's children). God made us such in order that we will tell the world about who He is and what He has done.

H

E

A

R

251//1 PETER 3–4

MEMORY VERSES: 1 PETER 2:11; 1 JOHN 4:10-11

After teaching how Christians are to behave amid persecution, Peter turned his attention to Christian wives and counseled them to submit to their husbands, to focus on inner purity rather than outer attire, and to extend goodwill toward others. He challenged husbands to honor their wives as having equal status spiritually. Peter also encouraged believers to get along with one another. They were to bless one another through sympathy, compassion, love, and humility. Repeatedly throughout his letter, Peter returned to the topic of suffering. The emphasis in chapter 4 is on sharing in Christ's suffering and resting in the promises that come through His victory over sin and death. With Christ as our example, we are to foster the same resolve Jesus had in regard to obeying God's will and loving and serving others. Because of the Holy Spirit's active presence in our lives, we are empowered both to endure suffering and to live for Christ.

As you read the Bible this week...

HIGHLIGHT the verses that speak to you.

Write out the name of the book:

Which chapter and verse numbers stand out to you?

EXPLAIN what this passage means.

To whom was it originally written? Why?

How does it fit with the verses before and after it?

What is the Holy Spirit intending to communicate through this text?

APPLY what God is saying in these verses to your life.

What does this mean today?

What is God saying to you personally?

How can you apply this message to your life?

RESPOND to what you've read.

In what ways does this passage call you to action?

How will you be different because of what you've learned?

Write out a prayer to God in response to what you read today:

252//1 PETER 5; 2 PETER 1

Peter closed his first letter by emphasizing the need for humility in every aspect of our lives, especially in our relationships. Peter warned against the rise of pride in one's life and expects all believers to relate to one another and to God in humility. His exhortation is especially important in light of the presence of the Devil, who actively targets Christians. Peter concluded his letter by encouraging Christians with the promise that the sovereign God would help them endure any trial that comes their way. While his first letter was meant to encourage believers in the midst of persecution, his second letter is written toward the general body of believers. It primarily emphasizes practical Christian living and growing in the knowledge of God. In the first chapter, Peter described the ideal character of a believer and provided proof for the trustworthiness of the gospel. A believer's life is to be rooted in his faith in God, which will grow as he or she practices it and seeks God as He has revealed Himself in Jesus Christ. The gospel that the apostles preached is a trustworthy source for this knowledge, and remains as true today as it was when they spoke it.

H

E

A

R

253//2 PETER 2–3

MEMORY VERSES: 1 PETER 2:11; 1 JOHN 4:10-11

In chapter 2, Peter explained why it is necessary to base our faith in God on the truth of the gospel: because there are counterfeiters among us. Coming at the church from the outside world was a barrage of heretical and blasphemous teachers and doctrines that had been dressed up to look like Christianity. Peter painted a scathing picture of these teachers. His language is rich with signs and warnings to avoid them at all costs and hold firm to the truth of the gospel that came from those who actually lived with and witnessed the teachings of Jesus. His examination of the false teachers reached a climax in chapter 3, where he reminded his readers to remember what the prophets and apostles of the Lord had spoken. He implored his readers to bear in mind the imminent return of our Lord, who will come like a thief in the night. The expectation of Jesus' return recalls the beginning of the letter, in which Peter urged believers to live upright, moral lives in full devotion to the teachings of Jesus Christ.

H

E

A

R

254//1 JOHN 1–3

MEMORY VERSES: 1 PETER 2:11; 1 JOHN 4:10-11

Like Peter's first letter, John's first letter is one of assurance and comfort to Christians. He began with a description of Jesus that emphasizes both His humanity and His divinity. Like Peter, John described the life of a follower of Christ, but he used the imagery of walking in the light to help us understand what the Christian life looks like. He finished the first chapter by encouraging us to reflect the light of our Heavenly Father through a morally pure lifestyle. In chapters 2 and 3, John described a believer's relationship as knowing Him personally. We display evidence of true knowledge of God by obeying His commands, walking as He walked, and loving others as He did. Because of his certainty at Christ's returning, John wrote that we must remain in Christ and remember His promise that He will return for us. Our love for others is modeled after Jesus' love for us, which is always sacrificial and costly.

H

E

A

R

255//1 JOHN 4–5

MEMORY VERSES: 1 PETER 2:11; 1 JOHN 4:10-11

Like Peter and Paul, John also addressed the issue of false teachers who were interfering with the spread of the gospel. Because of the very real and dangerous threat false teachings pose to believers' faith, John urged his readers to test all human teachers who claimed to speak with spiritual authority by the Word of God. The mark of genuine faith is the confession that Jesus Christ has come in the flesh. The truth about the nature of Christ is so basic to Christianity that it can never be compromised. Jesus is both fully God and fully man. The false teachers denied that Jesus came in the flesh. John abruptly turned from his discussion of true and false spirits to an appeal for believers to love one another once again. Christians should love one another because God has loved them first. God's supreme demonstration of love is seen in the sending of His Son as a sacrifice for our sins. In chapter 5, John summarized his letter by calling us to lives of obedience, love, and belief— belief in Jesus as the Christ, love for God and for one another, and obedience to God's commands.

H

E

A

R

256//REVELATION 1

MEMORY VERSES: REVELATION 3:19; REVELATION 21:3-4

The Bible begins with a picture of creation where God gave shape and life to the world and established His relationship with humanity. After sin entered the world, that relationship was broken. The rest of Scripture describes the great lengths God has gone to in order to draw people back to Himself. In the Book of Revelation, the final book of the Bible, we get a glimpse of the end days—the time when Jesus returns, God completes His redemptive work, and those who believe in Him receive final victory over sin and eternal life with Him. The apostle John, the author of Revelation, begins with a vision of Jesus that proves Jesus is alive and portrays a glory far beyond what we could ever imagine. John's response to this vision of Jesus shows us that Jesus deserves our worship. The more we understand who He is, the better we will understand how to worship Him.

As you read the Bible this week...

HIGHLIGHT the verses that speak to you.

Write out the name of the book:

Which chapter and verse numbers stand out to you?

EXPLAIN what this passage means.

To whom was it originally written? Why?

How does it fit with the verses before and after it?

What is the Holy Spirit intending to communicate through this text?

APPLY what God is saying in these verses to your life.

What does this mean today?

What is God saying to you personally?

How can you apply this message to your life?

RESPOND to what you've read.

In what ways does this passage call you to action?

How will you be different because of what you've learned?

Write out a prayer to God in response to what you read today:

257//REVELATION 2–3

MEMORY VERSES: REVELATION 3:19; REVELATION 21:3-4

Before Jesus showed John a vision of the end times, He gave him messages to send to seven churches located in present-day Turkey. Chapters 2 and 3 contain those letters. John had been pastor of the church of Ephesus, one of the seven, and had probably traveled extensively throughout the entire region visiting the people of these churches. His rapport with these churches would have likely made them listen to the words of the letters, even if they were harsh (as they sometimes are). At the center of each of the letters is one central call that remains important to us today: Remain true to the risen Christ regardless of your present circumstances. In each of the letters Jesus dictates to John, it is evident that He knows the people at these churches well. He was intimately familiar with their motivations, their strengths, and their weaknesses. In the same way, Jesus knows us well. When we become aware of God's knowledge of us, we are forced to confront our sins and rejoice for His mercy and grace.

H

E

A

R

258//REVELATION 4–5

After receiving the letters to the seven churches, John had a vision with two parts—a setting (chapter 4) and a series of events (chapters 5–8). According to chapter 4, the setting of this vision is the throne room of Heaven, which John described in intricate detail. Each of the characters represented in the vision are vividly portrayed and are shown to be worshiping the One on the throne forever. Rich in allusions to the Old Testament, particularly Ezekiel 1:5-10 and Isaiah 6, the picture of the throne room validated the things John would describe next. An accurate portrayal of heaven proves that he is a genuine prophet who speaks with divine authority. In chapter 5, John tells us what is going on. The One on the throne is holding a scroll in His right hand, but John weeps because nobody is worthy to even look at what it says. His tears do not last long, however, for the Lion of the Tribe of Judah, who has the appearance of a slaughtered Passover lamb, proves His worthiness to take the scroll and open it. The entire throne room falls down and worships Him just before He will open the seals one by one.

H

E

A

R

259//REVELATION 18–19

MEMORY VERSES: REVELATION 3:19; REVELATION 21:3-4

Chapters 18 and 19 detail John's vision of the fall of Babylon and the defeat of the Beast and his armies. Babylon, which is used throughout Revelation to refer to the system of the world which has organized in rebellion against God, is the subject of chapter 18. This "Great City" built for itself immense wealth and conducted itself with blasphemous arrogance in the face of God. In language that echoes Jeremiah 50-51, John recorded the song of victory sung by an Angel whose splendor illuminates the earth. In contrast to this Angel's victorious song, the world mourns for its "Great City" that has been laid to waste. Chapter 19 continues the celebration begun by the magnificent Angel, and a vast multitude in heaven rejoices at God's victory. God is a God who avenges injustice. John then witnesses the announcement of a wedding ceremony between the Lamb and His bride as He rides in on a white horse, clothed in brilliant white. With Jesus' entry to claim victory over Babylon, John witnesses the final defeat over the Beast and his armies. As Christians, we find strength and hope for life by realizing that when Jesus comes again He will defeat the forces of evil. This truth should also compel us to share the hope we have in Christ with everyone we know so they can share in the same promise.

H

E

A

R

260//REVELATION 20–22

The last chapters of Revelation focus on two things: Satan's final push and ultimate defeat, and a look ahead to our eternal future with God. In chapter 20, John described how Satan will be bound for a time and then will make one last push against God before being thrown into hell forever. We are being drawn constantly back to God's sovereignty and the hope that we have in His ultimate victory over sin, death, and hell. Chapter 21 begins the description of the new heaven, new earth, and new Jerusalem—a holy city. Time and again in Scripture we have seen how both creation and humanity were broken by sin, and here we see that God once and for all makes all things new, just as He promised. John closed his book in chapter 22 with a description of the river of life, which symbolizes the eternal life Jesus makes available for us. Just as the Bible began with a description of Eden, which fell, it ends with this description of a new Eden, which will endure forever because of Jesus' redemptive work. As Jesus wrapped up His vision to John, He issued an urgent call to faith. He desires that all people come to know Him. But a time is coming when unbelievers will have no hope of redemption from their sin and no offer of eternal life with God. Until then, God wants to use you to help those around you know Him personally.

H

E

A

R

SAMPLE H.E.A.R. ENTRY

Sample H.E.A.R. Journal

Read: Philippians 4:10-13   Date: 12-22-15   Title: Secret of Contentment

H (Highlight) "I am able to do all things through Him who strengthens me" (Phil. 4:13).

E (Explain) Paul was telling the church at Philippi that he has discovered the secret of contentment. No matter the situation in Paul's life, he realized that Christ was all he needed, and Christ was the one who strengthened him to persevere through difficult times.

A (Apply) In my life, I will experience many ups and downs. My contentment is not found in circumstances. Rather, it is based on my relationship with Jesus Christ. Only Jesus gives me the strength I need to be content in every circumstance of life.

R (Respond) Lord Jesus, please help me as I strive to be content in You. Through Your strength, I can make it through any situation I must face.

SAMPLE PRAYER LOG

Date Asked	Prayer Request	Date Answered

You then, my child, be strengthened bythe grace that is in Christ Jesus, and what you have heard from me in the presence of many witnesses entrust to faithful men who will be able to teach others also.

2 Timothy 2:2

F260 BIBLE READING PLAN

WEEK 1
- ❏ Genesis 1–2
- ❏ Genesis 3–4
- ❏ Genesis 6–7
- ❏ Genesis 8–9
- ❏ Job 1–2

MEMORY VERSES:
Genesis 1:27
Hebrews 11:7

WEEK 2
- ❏ Job 38–39
- ❏ Job 40–42
- ❏ Genesis 11–12
- ❏ Genesis 15
- ❏ Genesis 16–17

MEMORY VERSES:
Hebrews 11:6,8-10

WEEK 3
- ❏ Genesis 18–19
- ❏ Genesis 20–21
- ❏ Genesis 22
- ❏ Genesis 24
- ❏ Genesis 25:19-34; 26

MEMORY VERSES:
Romans 4:20-22
Hebrews 11:17-19

WEEK 4
- ❏ Genesis 27–28
- ❏ Genesis 29–30:24
- ❏ Genesis 31–32
- ❏ Genesis 33; 35
- ❏ Genesis 37

MEMORY VERSES:
2 Corinthians 10:12
1 John 3:18

WEEK 5
- ❏ Genesis 39–40
- ❏ Genesis 41
- ❏ Genesis 42–43
- ❏ Genesis 44–45
- ❏ Genesis 46–47

MEMORY VERSES:
Romans 8:28-30
Ephesians 3:20-21

WEEK 6
- ❏ Genesis 48–49
- ❏ Genesis 50–Exodus 1
- ❏ Exodus 2–3
- ❏ Exodus 4–5
- ❏ Exodus 6–7

MEMORY VERSES:
Genesis 50:20
Hebrews 11:24-26

WEEK 7

- ❏ Exodus 8–9
- ❏ Exodus 10–11
- ❏ Exodus 12
- ❏ Exodus 13:17–14
- ❏ Exodus 16–17

MEMORY VERSES:
John 1:29
Hebrews 9:22

WEEK 8

- ❏ Exodus 19–20
- ❏ Exodus 24–25
- ❏ Exodus 26–27
- ❏ Exodus 28–29
- ❏ Exodus 30–31

MEMORY VERSES:
Exodus 20:1-3
Galatians 5:14

WEEK 9

- ❏ Exodus 32–33
- ❏ Exodus 34–36:1
- ❏ Exodus 40
- ❏ Leviticus 8–9
- ❏ Leviticus 16–17

MEMORY VERSES:
Exodus 33:16
Matthew 22:37-39

WEEK 10

- ❏ Leviticus 23
- ❏ Leviticus 26
- ❏ Numbers 11–12
- ❏ Numbers 13–14
- ❏ Numbers 16–17

MEMORY VERSES:
Leviticus 26:13
Deuteronomy 31:7-8

WEEK 11

- ❏ Numbers 20; 27:12-23
- ❏ Numbers 34–35
- ❏ Deuteronomy 1–2
- ❏ Deuteronomy 3–4
- ❏ Deuteronomy 6–7

MEMORY VERSES:
Deuteronomy 4:7; 6:4-9

WEEK 12

- ❏ Deuteronomy 8–9
- ❏ Deuteronomy 30–31
- ❏ Deuteronomy 32:48-52; 34
- ❏ Joshua 1–2
- ❏ Joshua 3–4

MEMORY VERSES:
Joshua 1:8-9
Psalm 1:1-2

WEEK 13

- ❏ Joshua 5:10-15; 6
- ❏ Joshua 7–8
- ❏ Joshua 23–24
- ❏ Judges 2–3
- ❏ Judges 4

MEMORY VERSES:
Joshua 24:14-15
Judges 2:12

WEEK 14

- ❏ Judges 6–7
- ❏ Judges 13–14
- ❏ Judges 15–16
- ❏ Ruth 1–2
- ❏ Ruth 3–4

MEMORY VERSES:
Psalm 19:14
Galatians 4:4-5

WEEK 15

- ❏ 1 Samuel 1–2
- ❏ 1 Samuel 3; 8
- ❏ 1 Samuel 9–10
- ❏ 1 Samuel 13–14
- ❏ 1 Samuel 15–16

MEMORY VERSES:
1 Samuel 15:22; 16:7

WEEK 16

- ❏ 1 Samuel 17–18
- ❏ 1 Samuel 19–20
- ❏ 1 Samuel 21–22
- ❏ Psalm 22; 1 Samuel 24–25:1
- ❏ 1 Samuel 28; 31

MEMORY VERSES:
1 Samuel 17:46-47
2 Timothy 4:17a

WEEK 17

- ❏ 2 Samuel 1; 2:1-7
- ❏ 2 Samuel 3:1; 5; Psalm 23
- ❏ 2 Samuel 6–7
- ❏ Psalm 18; 2 Samuel 9
- ❏ 2 Samuel 11–12

MEMORY VERSES:
Psalms 23:1-3; 51:10-13

WEEK 18

- ❏ Psalm 51
- ❏ 2 Samuel 24; Psalm 24
- ❏ Psalm 1; 19
- ❏ Psalms 103; 119:1-48
- ❏ Psalm 119:49-128

MEMORY VERSES:
Psalms 1:1-7; 119:7-11

WEEK 19

- ❑ Psalms 119:129-176; 139
- ❑ Psalms 148–150
- ❑ 1 Kings 2
- ❑ 1 Kings 3; 6
- ❑ 1 Kings 8; 9:1-9

MEMORY VERSES:
Psalms 139:1-3; 139:15-16

WEEK 20

- ❑ Proverbs 1–2
- ❑ Proverbs 3–4
- ❑ Proverbs 16–18
- ❑ Proverbs 31
- ❑ 1 Kings 11–12

MEMORY VERSES:
Proverbs 1:7; 3:5-6

WEEK 21

- ❑ 1 Kings 16:29-34; 17
- ❑ 1 Kings 18–19
- ❑ 1 Kings 21–22
- ❑ 2 Kings 2
- ❑ 2 Kings 5; 6:1-23

MEMORY VERSES:
Psalm 17:15; 63:1

WEEK 22

- ❑ Jonah 1–2
- ❑ Jonah 3–4
- ❑ Hosea 1–3
- ❑ Amos 1:1; 9
- ❑ Joel 1–3

MEMORY VERSES:
Psalm 16:11
John 11:25-26

WEEK 23

- ❑ Isaiah 6; 9
- ❑ Isaiah 44–45
- ❑ Isaiah 52–53
- ❑ Isaiah 65–66
- ❑ Micah 1; 4:6-13; 5

MEMORY VERSES:
Isaiah 53:5-6
1 Peter 2:23-24

WEEK 24

- ❑ 2 Kings 17–18
- ❑ 2 Kings 19–21
- ❑ 2 Kings 22–23
- ❑ Jeremiah 1–3:5
- ❑ Jeremiah 25; 29

MEMORY VERSES:
Proverbs 29:18
Jeremiah 1:15

WEEK 25

- ❏ Jeremiah 31:31-40; 32–33
- ❏ Jeremiah 52; 2 Kings 24–25
- ❏ Ezekiel 1:1-3; 36:16-38; 37
- ❏ Daniel 1–2
- ❏ Daniel 3

MEMORY VERSES:
Ezekiel 36:26-27
Daniel 4:35

WEEK 26

- ❏ Daniel 5–6
- ❏ Daniel 9–10; 12
- ❏ Ezra 1–2
- ❏ Ezra 3–4
- ❏ Ezra 5–6

MEMORY VERSES:
Daniel 6:26-27; 9:19

WEEK 27

- ❏ Zechariah 1:1-6; 2; 12
- ❏ Ezra 7–8
- ❏ Ezra 9–10
- ❏ Esther 1–2
- ❏ Esther 3–4

MEMORY VERSES:
Zephaniah 3:17
1 Peter 3:15

WEEK 28

- ❏ Esther 5–7
- ❏ Esther 8–10
- ❏ Nehemiah 1–2
- ❏ Nehemiah 3–4
- ❏ Nehemiah 5–6

MEMORY VERSES:
Deuteronomy 29:29
Psalm 101:3-4

WEEK 29

- ❏ Nehemiah 7–8
- ❏ Nehemiah 9
- ❏ Nehemiah 10
- ❏ Nehemiah 11
- ❏ Nehemiah 12

MEMORY VERSES:
Nehemiah 6:9
Nehemiah 9:6

WEEK 30

- ❏ Nehemiah 13
- ❏ Malachi 1
- ❏ Malachi 2
- ❏ Malachi 3
- ❏ Malachi 4

MEMORY VERSES:
Psalm 51:17
Colossians 1:19-20

WEEK 31

- [ ] Luke 1
- [ ] Luke 2
- [ ] Matthew 1–2
- [ ] Mark 1
- [ ] John 1

MEMORY VERSES:
John 1:1-2,14

WEEK 32

- [ ] Matthew 3–4
- [ ] Matthew 5
- [ ] Matthew 6
- [ ] Matthew 7
- [ ] Matthew 8

MEMORY VERSES:
Matthew 5:16; 6:33

WEEK 33

- [ ] Luke 9:10-62
- [ ] Mark 9
- [ ] Luke 12
- [ ] John 3–4
- [ ] Luke 14

MEMORY VERSES:
Luke 14:26-27,33

WEEK 34

- [ ] John 6
- [ ] Matthew 19:16-30
- [ ] Luke 15–16
- [ ] Luke 17:11-37; 18
- [ ] Mark 10

MEMORY VERSES:
Mark 10:45
John 6:37

WEEK 35

- [ ] John 11; Matthew 21:1-13
- [ ] John 13
- [ ] John 14–15
- [ ] John 16
- [ ] Matthew 24:1-31

MEMORY VERSES:
John 13:34-35; 15:4-5

WEEK 36

- [ ] Matthew 24:32-51
- [ ] John 17
- [ ] Matthew 26:47–27:31
- [ ] Matthew 27:32-66; Luke 23:26-56
- [ ] John 19

MEMORY VERSES:
Luke 23:34
John 17:3

WEEK 37

- [ ] Mark 16
- [ ] Luke 24
- [ ] John 20–21
- [ ] Matthew 28
- [ ] Acts 1

MEMORY VERSES:
Matthew 28:18-20
Acts 1:8

WEEK 38

- [ ] Acts 2–3
- [ ] Acts 4–5
- [ ] Acts 6
- [ ] Acts 7
- [ ] Acts 8–9

MEMORY VERSES:
Acts 2:42; 4:31

WEEK 39

- [ ] Acts 10–11
- [ ] Acts 12
- [ ] Acts 13–14
- [ ] James 1–2
- [ ] James 3–5

MEMORY VERSES:
James 1:2-4; 2:17

WEEK 40

- [ ] Acts 15–16
- [ ] Galatians 1–3
- [ ] Galatians 4–6
- [ ] Acts 17–18:17
- [ ] 1 Thessalonians 1–2

MEMORY VERSES:
Acts 17:11,24-25

WEEK 41

- [ ] 1 Thessalonians 3–5
- [ ] 2 Thessalonians 1–3
- [ ] Acts 18:18-28; 19
- [ ] 1 Corinthians 1–2
- [ ] 1 Corinthians 3–4

MEMORY VERSES:
1 Corinthians 1:18
1 Thessalonians 5:23-24

WEEK 42

- [ ] 1 Corinthians 5–6
- [ ] 1 Corinthians 7–8
- [ ] 1 Corinthians 9–10
- [ ] 1 Corinthians 11–12
- [ ] 1 Corinthians 13–14

MEMORY VERSES:
1 Corinthians 10:13; 13:13

WEEK 43

- ❑ 1 Corinthians 15–16
- ❑ 2 Corinthians 1–2
- ❑ 2 Corinthians 3–4
- ❑ 2 Corinthians 5–6
- ❑ 2 Corinthians 7–8

MEMORY VERSES:
Romans 1:16-17
1 Corinthians 15:3-4

WEEK 44

- ❑ 2 Corinthians 9–10
- ❑ 2 Corinthians 11–13
- ❑ Romans 1–2; Acts 20:1-3
- ❑ Romans 3–4
- ❑ Romans 5–6

MEMORY VERSES:
Romans 5:1
2 Corinthians 10:4

WEEK 45

- ❑ Romans 7–8
- ❑ Romans 9–10
- ❑ Romans 11–12
- ❑ Romans 13–14
- ❑ Romans 15–16

MEMORY VERSES:
Romans 8:1; 12:1-2

WEEK 46

- ❑ Acts 20–21
- ❑ Acts 22–23
- ❑ Acts 24–25
- ❑ Acts 26–27
- ❑ Acts 28

MEMORY VERSES:
Acts 20:24
2 Corinthians 4:7-10

WEEK 47

- ❑ Colossians 1–2
- ❑ Colossians 3–4
- ❑ Ephesians 1–2
- ❑ Ephesians 3–4
- ❑ Ephesians 5–6

MEMORY VERSES:
Ephesians 2:8-10
Colossians 2:6-7

WEEK 48

- ❑ Philippians 1–2
- ❑ Philippians 3–4
- ❑ Hebrews 1–2
- ❑ Hebrews 3–4
- ❑ Hebrews 5–6

MEMORY VERSES:
Philippians 3:7-8
Hebrews 4:14-16

WEEK 49

- ❏ Hebrews 7
- ❏ Hebrews 8–9
- ❏ Hebrews 10
- ❏ Hebrews 11
- ❏ Hebrews 12

MEMORY VERSES:
Galatians 2:19-20
2 Corinthians 5:17

WEEK 50

- ❏ 1 Timothy 1–3
- ❏ 1 Timothy 4–6
- ❏ 2 Timothy 1–2
- ❏ 2 Timothy 3–4
- ❏ 1 Peter 1–2

MEMORY VERSES:
2 Timothy 2:1-2,15

WEEK 51

- ❏ 1 Peter 3–4
- ❏ 1 Peter 5; 2 Peter 1
- ❏ 2 Peter 2–3
- ❏ 1 John 1–3
- ❏ 1 John 4–5

MEMORY VERSES:
1 Peter 2:11
1 John 4:10-11

WEEK 52

- ❏ Revelation 1
- ❏ Revelation 2–3
- ❏ Revelation 4–5
- ❏ Revelation 18–19
- ❏ Revelation 20–22

MEMORY VERSES:
Revelation 3:19; 21:3-4

NOTES

Disciple-Making Resources

Replicate.org

Our Replicate website is packed with tools to help create awareness for disciple-making. In addition to downloads and web-based content, the Replicate blog is a great source of insight and commentary on the current state of disciple-making.

Weekly Long Hollow Facebook Live

Each week Pastor Robby broadcasts live on Facebook Live with a 30-minute walk through the Word. Each broadcast dives deeper into the Foundations reading plan and answers live questions about God's Word. Tune in on Facebook each Tuesday at 2pm central time at facebook.com/longhollow.

The Growing Up Series

01 Growing Up. *Growing Up* is a practical, easy-to-implement system for growing in one's faith. It is a manual for making disciples, addressing the what, why, where, and how of discipleship. *Growing Up* provides you with transferrable principles for creating and working with discipleship groups, allowing you to gain positive information both for yourself and for others as you learn how to help others become better disciples for Christ.

02 Firmly Planted. Why Is spiritual growth complicated? *Firmly Planted* is the second book in the Growing Up series. In biblical, practical, and simple terms, the book shares a roadmap for spiritual maturity. *Firmly Planted* addresses topics such as how you can be sure of your salvation, why your identity in Christ affects everything you do, how to overcome the three enemies that cripple a Christian's growth, a battle plan for gaining victory over temptation, and the indispensable spiritual discipline every believer must foster.

03 Bearing Fruit. *Bearing Fruit* is the third book in the Growing Up series. In this book, the reader will understand how God grows believers. Robby identifies seven places the word "fruit" is found in the bible: fruit of holiness, fruit of righteousness, fruit of soul-winning, fruit of the spirit, fruit of the praise, fruit of repentance, and fruit of giving. You will understand your role in the fruit bearing process of spiritual growth. *Bearing Fruit* is applicable for new and mature believers alike.

ESSENTIAL
TEEN STUDY BIBLE

The HCSB Essential Teen Study Bible can give teens all the tools needed to tackle this life and learn to live it God's way. Filled with hundreds of study helps and 146 devotions written especially for teens, this fully designed, four-color Bible will help them apply God's Word each day and connect with Him as never before.